THE REAL CASES OF DETECTIVE TOMASSI

15 Real Stories of Murder and Robbery Cases Solved with Forensic Science

Clive Loxley

Dear Reader,

This is the first volume in a series of books that brings to fruition the work of a detective over several decades.

All stories present true cases, therefore the names of all locations as well as the names of the characters have been changed to protect the identities of the people involved.

Sincerely,
The Author

TABLE OF CONTENTS

01

MY
MENTORS

MY MENTORS

In the autumn of 1975, when I graduated from the Officer Candidate School, I was appointed to work at the police headquarters in X city. My colleagues there were the ones who trained me best for the work I did. I thank everyone, but especially my mentor, Officer Smith, who became my model. I did my best to be like him, but I must admit that I could not surpass him. I will try to depict the way this man influenced me the best I can. Apart from him, two other infallible forensic officers guided me through my first cases. They are Captain Floyd and Captain Decker.

They mastered methods of revealing the traces at the crime scene, forensic photography and forensic expertise of most traces discovered at the crime scene. They often tested me on what I knew in the field of forensics. I liked that they appreciated me for having more theoretical knowledge than them. Even from the first case, when I returned from the scene with digital traces and matters, they praised me.

We had a positive working environment, with mutual respect and appreciation. However, they were dissatisfied that the merits of their work were not appreciated by their colleagues, even though many of the cases had been solved due to them. I told them that in order to solve this discontentment, they should write down their ideas and send them for publication in the magazines edited by the police.

"And who will write those?", Captain Floyd asked me.

"You", I replied, "Mr. Decker and if you want it, me too."

"We would be delighted," said Mr. Floyd.

I must admit, that exhortation was enough for me. Later, I wrote and sent for publication a number of their achievements under my signature. When I as they would have never written forensic articles. I will tell you about two of the cases they were proud of in the following lines.

Officer Floyd told me that a few years before, he was part of the on-site research team, who went to B. city to search the house of a woman missing from home. It was a middle-aged deaf-mute woman, who was living alone, working as a textile spinner at the factory in the city. Officer Moore from the Coroner's Office, was also part of the team. The woman was not found and in such situations, fingerprints, documents and photographs that will be used later to establish the identities of people or corpses with unknown identity are sought.

Officer Moore, while investigating among the acquaintances and neighbors of the missing person, established that she had previously lived with a man, who was also deaf-mute. After some time and investigations, the officer managed to identify this man, who was currently in the C. police custody, being investigated for a criminal offense committed against another deaf-mute woman. The investigation of this suspect was quite difficult due to the disabilities he had, but also because of the meanness and obstinacy he manifested towards the investigator. All they could get from him was that he knew nothing about his former mistress, R.S. He admitted having lived with her for some time, but at one point they did not get along anymore and they broke up.

My colleague attached the sheet with the fingerprints and the identification photos of the deaf-mute to the case file. The investigations in this case stagnated for a while, which is why the Jewish community in C. city expressed their dissatisfaction, because the missing person was part of that community. The case was re-analyzed at the command of the Local Police and a significant number of informative activities, but also re-searching the house of the missing person were ordered.

The detective arrived again in the house of the missing woman and this time, the result of the research led to the case resolution. "When I opened the doors leading to the stairs towards the cellar," Officer Floyd told me, "a musty smell hit me in the face. I went down the wooden steps and in the light of the flashlight I found a sand mound on the floor. In the mound there were several glass shards, probably coming from the window glass located on the wall opposite the entrance to the cellar.

For the success of the research I brought a projector in the cellar, in the light of which I carefully raised the glass shards and examined them "contrejour" I found the presence of several digital traces that were revealed with quartz powder. Someone had put these pieces upright. I found this because probably the one who put them wanted to hide what we found in the sand. When we removed the sand, the body of a woman who was not rotten was found, the tissues being dried. I was convinced that I solved the case and continued the story of Officer Floyd. When I compared the digital traces on the glass chunks and the typical impressions, a comparative model on the deaf-mute sheet.

It was a great success for the Police of the city of S. a lot was written about the merits of the investigators, but about us, the criminals, nothing was written; The investigation and investigations were important ".

The second case of my colleagues' dissatisfaction was related to a murder that had been committed during a brawl between a group of men in a commune near the city of D. Officer Decker, who had been present at the on-site research, told me that the merit in identifying the criminal divides him with the forensic.

In the reported case, it was about several young people, leaving the bar of the village, starting a fight, hitting each other with fists, sticks and cutting objects. It all ended when one of them fell to the ground, with a bloody face. The brawlers fled, hiding as far away from the place. Even though the identity of the brawlers had been established, it was impossible to determine who was the one who applied the death-causing blow. The one who was dead in front of the jail had an ellipsoidal blow in the occipital area, from where a lot of blood had flowed. During the autopsy the prosecutor and the judicial officer were changing opinions on the difficulty of the investigation. It was mentioned that it was a "Rix", when the guilt of the participants in the beating cannot be established.

In such cases, all participants receive the same punishment. What followed was not a case of "Rix", because absolutely by chance, the result of autopsy and traceology expertise led to the identification of the one who applied the death -causing blow.

When the victim's cranial vault was cut open and the coroner examined the cerebral matter, he found that a metal fragment was detached from the table and got stuck to the scalpel. Carefully examined, it was found that this metal fragment was present on one of the edges, in the shape of a crescent; the peculiarities of breaking and detaching it from the metal body of which it had been part. It was guessed that the fragment came from the edge of an ax with a narrow blade. To determine where this fragment came from, searches were carried out at the homes of those who participated in the fight. Axes with smaller or larger blades, which were examined in the area of the edges were taken from them. In one of them, a crescent-shaped area was discovered, where a metal portion was missing.

When the fragment was placed next to the crescent area, it was found that the combination was perfect, demonstrating that through its linear continuity, the ax cut and the metal fragment made a common body. No one, until then, had highlighted the significance of such a forensic demonstration.

I asked Officer Decker to agree to publish this case in the specialized magazine and he accepted. I must admit that later I participated in different meetings and symposiums of forensics, which were a continuation of the cases I had exposed. These and the ones that followed represent for me the dense mass of my professional satisfaction. At the same time, I am pleased that through my reports, I made them stand out, becoming known as true professionals.

***

02

THE ACCIDENT

THE ACCIDENT

Every time I go through the S. village, on my way to T.,whenever I pass by the building that was once(and maybe still is) a winery, I remember a car accident that I was involved in solving.

I also remember two of the ex-mates that were at the on-site investigation with me, further necessary investigations, identification of the vehicle involved and of course the driver who had done a hit and run.

It was the fall of 1982, in the evening, when a truck coming on the road from the outskirts of the village, hit a two-horse cart from behind. After the impact, the carter was thrown (the carter- a man from the village) on the road, and died instantly.

The coat was severely damaged, a horse was killed and the other one was lying on the side of the road. When we arrived at the scene, there were several traces on the road known in the literature as "matters/materials".

I remember seeing fragments of the cart wood, the blood of the horses, plenty of colorless glass shards and pieces of yellow plastic and blue paint films.The latter had various shapes and sizes, probably coming from the truck involved in the accident. One of my mates told me :

"Tomassi, let's get this over with, not only that it's getting dark, but look at the long lines of cars in both directions!

In both directions there were indeed two long lines of vehicles stopped, waiting for the traffic to be resumed. I tried to do my job as fast as I could, but I had to follow all the necessary steps: that is, to take photos of the crime scene, every trace (in detail), to collect specimens and pack them in paper envelopes, to make a provisional sketch of the place.

I took photos of the cart and horses as they were positioned. The carter had already been sent to the hospital. When traffic was resumed, we were all in the area between the road and the fence of the winery and we were reviewing the results at the scene.

While discussing, we were rapidly informed by the constable who, in his turn, had got a hint that the truck involved in the accident was driven by the Hester driver, living in the village. I asked him who had informed him and he replied he had his sources.

"What kind of sources", I asked him.

"It's someone living here by the road and who saw the truck drive by Hester passing. He didn't see the accident happening, but he heard the noise made by the impact.

"But that isn't a source of information!" I contradicted him. That's a witness.

"Well, he doesn't want to be a witness. He informed me, but insisted on not including him as a witness in this thing."

"Well, if this is how things are, let's find the truck. Where can we find it ?"

"Let's get to the driver's house", said the constable.

After a while, we reached the driver's yard, but the truck was not there. After searching all the corners of the wide yard, the constable told us :

"I know this driver is kind of a boozer/drunkard. He might have taken the truck to his grandfather's yard, which is situated somewhere on the outskirts of the village.

And he was right. We found the truck hidden between two haystacks, where his grandfather had a stable for the cattle. On examining the truck, after putting the hay aside, we found the truck had signs of slight deformation, the right side headlight was broken and there were glass fragments inside it.

The turn signal on the same side was in the same condition, with fragments of yellow plastin inside it, too. The engine hood was deformed and paint missing in some parts of it. It was all clear to me.

It was simple to demonstrate this was the truck involved in the accident. I took a general photo of the truck as it was, and then of each detail of the traces on the car body. We attached the paint fragments from the accident site, the shards of glass and yellow plastic in the areas where they were missing.

Their shapes fitted perfectly with their margins on the body of the car. It was quite uncomplicated (when I reached the lab) to make photographic plates to prove the identity of the truck involved in the accident.

All these details are part of the Forensic chapter of traceology, where "dynamic" but also "shape" traces are used to reconstruct the whole. This method is unbeatable in proving the identity of the objects used in committing crimes.

The more difficult, the more non-linear the breaking directions, the higher the degree of precision. In this case, these identification possibilities undoubtedly convinced everyone involved in establishing the truth.

For me, a newly arrived in the police force, compared to the other policemen, this accident was another moment of appreciation and satisfaction.

***

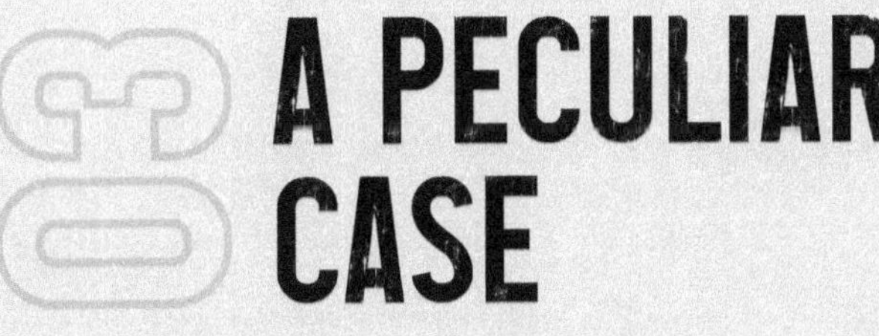

03

A PECULIAR CASE

A PECULIAR CASE

I have faced many murder cases. The number of murders is lower compared to other types of crimes, but they make strong waves in the community. In their anatomy, the worst ways of killing I have encountered had happened within homosexual groups.

The violence, I can say, even the brutality of the deed stands apart from the other categories of murder. I can think of a case that was not a homicide (because the victim was taken to the hospital immediately and saved) when a man was discovered one September morning in an unimaginable situation.

The man was lying on the ground (somewhere in the back of a bowling alley), naked, with his genitals missing. I recall that the coroner stated in his autopsy report that the injury was caused by flaying the scrotum and the phallus altogether. The victim survived thanks to Dr. Grant, head of the urology department at the county hospital.

He attached to the victim, through plastic surgery an artificial urethra so that he could urinate. I will not refer to this case, but to another one, which, through its originality, made the identification of the author different from the classical methods of identification.

At the beginning of the 90s, I saw myself facing a wave of violent crimes such as robberies, burglaries and last but not least, thefts of cars and from cars. We considered that everything happened within the city and for this fact, we thought we had to check the vehicles and suspicious people coming in and out of the city on all access routes. I was right.

The checkpoints we established, through the officers on duty, during the checks carried out quite often discovered people who were leaving the city with stolen goods or were fugitives. Oftentimes, when meeting some of the people I knew, I was scolded that on the travels they had made to other cities, they were not stopped for control as it happened in our city.

The case I am referring to is an example of demonstrating the effectiveness of this measure. Even if it was extreme, it was still due to the unfortunate situation of criminality at that time. To check the efficiency of the services in the checking points, I and my subordinate colleagues, heads of departments, checked day and night, the way the agents carried out these checks. Many of their findings were guided by us, coordinating them in the execution of procedural documents for the swift conclusion of the investigations.

We had a special room in the Police headquarters, where we would keep those who, for various reasons, did not stop at the officers' signals, and whose investigation was to be carried out in the first hours after their arrest. One morning, around 6:00 a.m., when I arrived at the Police headquarters to check on the officers' shift change, I was told by the unit duty officer that law enforcement officers from one of the newly established checkpoints managed to detain a young man who had not stopped at their signal. In the investigation room, I saw a young man around 20-25 years old, handcuffed, with his hands behind his back, sitting on the bench inside the room. The NCO who was supervising him reported the following to me:

"Around 3 in the morning, I saw a car coming from the city with its headlights on. From the way it was moving, with sudden starts and stops, I suspected that it had engine problems. When it got close to us, I signaled him to stop, but if we hadn't jumped to the sides, he would have run over me and my companion as well. It was a blue car, which continued its way with the engine coughing, stopping somewhere 200 m away in the middle of the road. I ran and I took this one out from behind the wheel of the car."

"Have you determined who he is?"

The one I was referring to started crying. I asked him:

"Why are you crying? Did they beat you?"

He shook his head nervously, tears streaming down his dirty cheeks. The NCO tells me he has no ID on him, refuses to say his name and won't say whose car it is.

"We were the ones to drive the car to the police yard and this is its key", the non-commissioned officer told me. "On the driver's seat I found this plastic bag with candy, gum, chocolate bars and a bottle of fizzy drink." I addressed the young man:

"Why didn't you stop at the officer's signal?"

He went on crying without saying anything. I ordered his handcuffs to be removed and a report to be drawn up, to mention the circumstances in which he was detained, and the Forensic Department to draw up a photographic plate with the following pictures: the photo of the car, of the goods in the bag and the detainee's face seen from the front and the straight profile. By lunchtime, the minutes and the photographic plate were drawn up.

When they were brought to me for verification, the criminal investigation officer reported to me that he still had to check the records of registered cars, to find out who owned the car. I can understand now that either what happened next was a fluke or that my checkpoint method was the best. After a few minutes, I was called by the head of the inspectorate, who, in a concerned voice, informed me that officers from the judicial service had been alerted to the fact that a citizen from C.

Street had been found dead in his apartment, in a state of putrefaction. He also informed me that when he went to that address, it was found that the person in question had head injuries and a metal hammer was found next to him in bed. The state of decay was obvious, the smell coming from the apartment disturbing the neighbors. "No one", the chief inspector continued to tell me, "noticed the tenant's absence, thinking he was gone, because his car was not in the parking lot." I asked him if he knew the license plate number of the car and what color it was. After a pause that seemed quite long to me (because I heard him talking to those around him), he informed me that it was a blue car with the same registration number as the car detained at the checkpoint. I told him that "I solved the case a few hours ago." The pause that followed seemed unnatural.

" What do you mean ?"

"I mean that the actual murderer and the car are right before my eyes."

He stopped answering my phone and in less than half an hour, he was in my office accompanied by three criminal investigation department officers. I told them how the events happened, and they, without doing any formality, took the young man, the documents we prepared and the car and they left. It wasn't the first time this happened. There was neither a "good job" nor a "thank you" line. I, on the other hand, thanked and congratulated the non-commissioned officers who had stopped the car. And to make good their success, I awarded them. What did I find out later? The young man, a worker, was waiting at the station for the train that would take him home.

He was hungry, upset that he couldn't find a job until he was approached by a not-too-old man and began a conversation with him. From the discussions with that man, he understood that he was a "good" man; he invited him to have a steak ,"a quick one" with 2-3 cold beers, telling him that he would help him find a job. He accepted the man's invitation to go to his house where he could not leave afterwards. After initially treating him well and dining together, he forced (constrained) him to have homosexual intercourse with him. He kept him there for several days, shoving him every time he tried to leave the apartment.

He stopped resisting and accepted all the caresses and intercourses he was subjected to. He waited until his "benefactor" fell asleep and taking advantage of this, he took a hammer that he had discovered in the apartment and violently applied several blows to his head. He left the apartment after taking the car key and money from the victim's wallet. He took the car from the parking lot, went to a few restaurants, waiting for nightfall to leave for home. However, he did not check if the fuel tank was full, this is how the engine malfunction was explained when he was seen by the policemen at the checkpoint. This case demonstrates the peculiarity of each investigation related to the personality of the murderer and the victim. There is no general recipe for a crime.

***

A FORENSIC OFFICER'S TENACITY

A FORENSIC OFFICER'S TENACITY

I often remember some of my colleagues I wasn't friends with; but in our work of uncovering criminals, a few stood out for their flair and tenacity. The one I am referring to now, I know little about his family life, and I do not wish to nominate him at this point. I will, perhaps, at the end of this literary attempt. I'm thinking of him because in the latter part of his police career he had overt displays of envy and malice towards me.

However, I can't help but appreciate him. When I came to X city, the most important characteristic of police work was that of great violence. Almost weekly, cases of men arriving at the hospital emergency room in a coma with injuries to their face and head were reported. Investigations revealed that those in question had been discovered in various places lying on the ground in a state of unconsciousness, with no money or valuables on them.

Most of these men were workers from the two large industrial units in the area. Almost all the victims who were brought to the hospital were drunk. I concluded this as a result of my experience, not because I might have found them in a statistic. The statistics were different. I described these because the man I am referring to actually impressed me not for the mentioned cases, but for others, each with a different specificity.

One April morning, the officer I'm talking about came into my office and asked me to accompany him to an on-site investigation into the robbery of a pensioner. At the crime scene, in the car he told me that he wanted me to do the on-site investigation and not my colleague, who was on duty that day.

I was pleased that he chose me; it was an appreciation coming from a legal expert who often paid a lot of attention to informative work rather than to forensics.

The present case was of a pensioner who had gone to the market, sent by his wife, to buy lamb. She had advised him to be careful not to be tricked by some seller into buying dog meat, as was then rumored to be practiced in the markets.

The husband promised to be careful and went to the market. But he never returned home. Only at dawn the next day was he discovered by his neighbors lying on the ground in front of his house. He was picked up by neighbors along with his wife, put in a neighbor's car and taken to the emergency room.

The medical staff called the police, and the interviews made by the officer clarified where the pensioner had been until then. On examination he was found to have a swollen face, fractured jaws with missing teeth, and a dental crown which the injured man had fitted several years before. Doctors in intensive care told the coroner that in their opinion he would not survive.

We go to where the victim was discovered by the neighbors. I'm thinking that whoever fractured his jaws inflicted his injuries when the victim was on the ground. "That's where I think we'll find clues", the officer explained to me.

He was right because there, the ground was soft, soaked with the blood that had flowed from his mouth. We found there two deep footprints. I remember them being quite clear, the ground faithfully retaining the characteristics of the footwear that created them.

My job was simple: I prepared a mixture of plaster and water, which I poured into those tracks. Until the plaster hardened (this was the casting method to collect the trace) I picked up fragments of soft soil which I inserted into a test tube. When we find the suspect, we'll examine his footwear, and besides the shape and size, who knows, we'll find soil residue on the footwear. My work was simple: the most important and substantial work was that of the officer.

After about a week, he informed me by phone that he found the one who committed the robbery, but to prove his guilt, he needed me. Because my lab was away from the police headquarters, I went there, where in an office, there was a handcuffed young man, tall and athletic, who looked at me indifferently when I entered the room. He was wearing a pair of short studded boots with high heels.

I asked the officer for the alleged culprit to take off his shoes and give me his boots. Then, in a dish, in which I had prepared soft yellow earth, I made deep marks with each boot; but after examining the soles, I discovered in the space between the heel and the sole, a fine layer of dry earth. I saw this dust and put it in a glass test tube.

After this, we found that the footprint at the scene had the same characteristics (dimensions) as the sole of the boot for the right foot. On the same day, the result of laboratory analysis comparing the soil taken from the scene and the dry soil from the suspect's boots contained traces of human blood of the same blood type.

I asked the officer how he got to the suspect. "It's a long story. The pensioner's wife told me that her husband used to drink at the restaurant in the square."

I went to the restaurant with the most recent photo of the victim and questioned the two barmaids there, showing them the photo of the victim. One of them told me that she knew him because he was a regular customer of the place. She remembered the last time he sat at a table with a younger man dressed in a black leather coat, as long as an overcoat. She remembered that they left the restaurant together.

"You're right", I say, "usually sellers, unlike other people, remember the faces of customers."

"This is what I also relied on, because with her, I "patrolled" with my team several days in a row in the market, on the adjacent streets, on the sidewalk in front of the restaurant, and in the end, she indicated the suspect to me when he entered a store.

It was hard enough to detain him. Did you see his hands? It's like they're shovels. If he had been a boxer, he would have been a Rocky Marciano. We had quite a hard time putting him down and handcuffing him."

"Who is he??"

"A welder."

"What does he state ?"

"Well, nothing, he does not want to speak. But it's ok, I'm going with him to the Prosecutor's Office, I get a warrant, I get him a public defender and I'll get it out of him.

And so it was, because less than half a day later, in the evening, I was in his apartment. I found nothing to incriminate him. Instead, the officer, like a true forensic officer, opened a manhole in the bathroom, under the sink, where the faucets of the hot and cold water pipes were placed, taking out a jar where there were among others: gold earrings, rings, wedding rings and a dental crown, which was not gold, but gaudent.

It was then that everyone in the search team understood how the dental crown had been removed from the pensioner's mouth. I'm sure this idiot kicked him in the mouth with his boots to get his crown off.

Later we found out that the pensioner had already died, and our suspect muttered, at the end of the interview that after putting the pensioner to the ground, he fractured his jaw.

After a certain period of time, as I was busy working on other cases too, I was visited by a journalist, who came to interview me about this case. I had been recommended to him by the officer to whom I refer. I refused to participate in the interview, saying that the credit was not mine. I looked at this officer in a new light and I remember another case, in which I did not participate, but which was also solved by him and his team. I compared the tenacity of this man to that of a bulldog, who when catching the thread of a case, does not let go until he reaches the end of it.

Here is the case: On a street behind the biggest store in town, in a house there lived a nurse. That assistant had been missing from work for several days.

He was discovered in the room he rented, dead, with signs of putrefaction. At the on-site investigation and examination of the body, it was found that the injuries that caused his death were due to repeated blows to the head with the sole of an athletic shoe. A pair of athletic shoes was found there, with traces of blood and hair on the metal spikes.

I learned that it was the same officer who discovered the perpetrators of the murder. His course of action consisted of questioning the owner of the building who stated that the victim was visited by two young men who stayed overnight to sleep.

Upon the officer's request if he could recognize the two, the owner agreed to accompany the police team to "have a walk" around the city, as in the previous example. The practice of this police method of identifying the perpetrators is well mastered by the police.

The officer was in the position of police spokesperson. Journalists ironically told him that instead of a spokesperson, he is the "tricky spokesman", not giving them the information they believed to be true for the ongoing cases.

Now that he is no longer with us, as I was retired, I had the pleasure of listening to one of the officers employed directly who confessed to me that he was the grandson of this officer.

His confession went like that:

"Remember ! Detective Tomassi is a real professional that I enjoyed working with."

I liked his words. I also thanked the officer up there, wherever he might be.

***

50

THE ABORTION

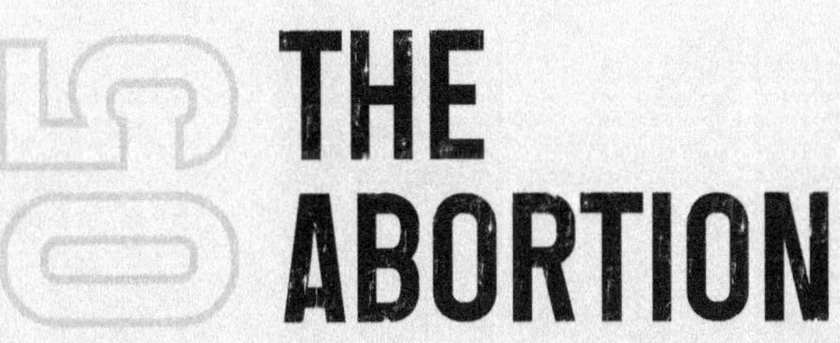

THE ABORTION

Many times as I was passing in my car to I., I would see a fountain with a shadoof and I would remember a case that I can compare to the story of Elia Kazan's movies. I am talking about the "America, America" movie, especially about the first scenes, where there are some landscapes in which the hero's life unfolds and they are similar to those that come to my mind now.

The well had a gutter next to it that was made from a cut and unfolded tire of a tractor. It was there that livestock keepers watered their thirsty animals. Around the well, the ground was dry, keeping the traces of the hoofs, smaller or larger, made by cattle and sheep. 40 years ago, when a shepherd came to water his sheep, they backed away in fear because a woman's body was lying near the gutter.

When the research team arrived at the crime scene it was found that there was the body of a young woman, scantily clad in a gray tergal fabric skirt and a T-shirt of the same color. Her head was uncovered, her hair cut short and in her right ear, she had an earring in the shape of a lily of the valley bloom. The left earlobe, although pierced, had no earring. No stockings on her legs, they were stretched straight side by side, and on her feet she had a pair of black rubber sneakers. Underneath, the corpse had no underwear; panties, top and bra missing.

The investigation did not last long and subsequently the identity of the deceased could not be established. Until the next day, despite all the investigations, it was not possible to find out who the woman in question was. The autopsy of the corpse did not reveal any traces of violence on the head, hands, legs and torso.

Only when the chest and groin area were opened, the medical examiner informed us that the woman was pregnant in the first month of pregnancy, and the uterus had a wound caused by stabbing with a hard object. He believed death had been caused by a gas embolism. The research did not progress because it was not possible to establish the identity of the victim for several days. Despite all the investigations carried out in the mentioned villages, no woman was missing from the home.

Variants were also considered about how the body was brought and abandoned near the well. Almost a week had passed since the discovery of the body and the investigation was back to square one. The only certainty was that, indeed, the death occurred due to some abortive maneuvers performed by unprepared people, who, through inadequate methods, perforated the victim's uterus, thus letting a quantity of air into the circulatory system.

This air enters the blood circuit of the heart and penetrated the body producing fibrillation and cardiac arrest. This is what the medical examiner explained to us, and this is where the research started to identify the author of the abortion.

"However, the author of the abortion cannot be a medical professional"; the doctor explained to us. "Certainly," he continued, it happened in one of the houses in the villages located in this area. The method and the means of transport used to bring the body to the field were important for the research.

After almost a month, the constable in one of the villages located further than the three villages, presented a piece of information stating that a former midwife from his village, years ago, was performing abortions on some women. The information was likely to be true, which is why a team consisting of a prosecutor, the criminal investigation officer and myself, the forensic scientist, went to the woman's home.

The house was similar to the other houses with several rooms, a porch in the front and the kitchen was made up of an appurtenance placed at the end of the house with an exit towards the not very large garden. The yard and the garden were proof that a man's hand was lacking in the household.

The woman was a widow over 70 years old, who had assisted the birth of many children in her youth. She was the suspect in our case. The search that was carried out did not reveal any suspicious objects, neither in the large room facing the street, where the bed was found with unused sheets, (proving that no one had slept there for a long time) nor in the closet located on the right side of the door.

Likewise in the common hall that opened into another room used as a bedroom. But, in the kitchen, on examining the cups in the wall cabinet (ceramic cups on which the names of the spices were written) an orange rubber bulb with a sharp point was found as well as a hose made of the same material. It was about 10 cm long, with a closed-end, which had a hole a few millimeters from the tip that connected to the cylindrical inner part of the 2-3 mm diameter tube.

On the dirt floor of the kitchen, covered with loom handmade mats, with the help of the strong light of the projector that he had in the kit, after a meticulous search, he found an earring in the shape of a lily of the valley bloom, somewhere under a backless sofa.

The rules of forensic tactics require that during the searches carried out in the houses located in a courtyard, all the spaces, garden covered and uncovered spaces as well as in the premises of the toilets that are in these courtyards should be checked.

With all the disgust and disgrace, using the services of a villager who for a certain financial facility, with metal rods, from the feces located here, he removed the clothing items. After they were washed right there in the yard with water from the well, it was found that they were a pair of panties, a bra and a top. I did not participate in the hearing of the old woman, but I later learned that she admitted that the victim's abortion had been performed in her kitchen.

This young woman came several times to her house, asking her to induce an abortion. She was asking for this because she had become pregnant from an adulterous relationship with a friend of her husband's that he knew about and was threatening her. At first, she did not agree with the termination of the pregnancy, but the amount of money offered was high enough for her to accept.

She thought that girl was unlucky because her method of causing an abortion was pretty well mastered and consisted of inserting a tube into the uterus, where, with the help of the bulb-shaped pump, she would insert warm water in the form of brine. Perhaps, if she had stood still while pumping the brine, she wouldn't have passed out, a faint from which she never awoke.

She tried to get rid of the body and it was difficult for her until she found a nephew, a drunkard, who would have been able to "kill even his mother " for booze. "I don't know where he took her.

He only came to take the other share of the money, telling me not to worry, that no one will know anything." She felt sorry for that girl. In order not to be discovered, she threw into the toilet the underwear that remained after removing the body from the house.

I was not interested in how and how many years in prison the two people got: the midwife and the drunken nephew. For me, what was important in this case was how our discovery and their punishment were done through a combination of the knowledge of the criminal investigation and forensic medicine.

***

06

A POLICE FORCE HERO

A POLICE FORCE HERO

Some criminological ideas come to mind when I think about the destiny of Lieutenant Wise, a police hero. In his memory and that of Officer Mann (another hero), the colleagues erected a small monument on the entrance alley of the police main headquarters in the city of H. Human communities are afraid of two great dangers: diseases and murders.

It is doctors and police officers who fight against them. The community has different attitudes toward the medical and police staff. We all found it different because while doctors are appreciated and paid, quite a few of them rarely are "doctors without silver", while the police officers, most of the times, are regarded with wickedness, considered uneducated, bad at heart and even considered "natural enemies" of their fellow citizens.

The rumor has plenty of jokes, ironies and funny stories about the latter. Our community is not prepared to carry out its activities to prevent and combat crime, unfairly considering " it is their job", that is, the state represented locally by the policemen. The communities are filled with unknown criminals, the creators of hidden criminality, being called by specialists "the black figure of crime".

Some of the criminals committing these acts in certain specific situations of life, almost for no reason, kill the policemen. Lieutenant Wise was a fresh graduate of the Police Academy. He was in his first years of activity in the field of combating generally reported offenses. He was appointed to deal with the fraud offenses department.

Among the hit-and-run cases he had dealt with, he found that there was something they all had in common; the author was the same woman who, taking advantage of the naivety of some families involved in burial procedures, offered her services for a fee to purchase goods, taking the money from

those concerned and disappearing to the organizers'
damage.

The officer was familiar with the working method
in such cases and had managed to get the identikit of
the offender. It was a working technique used by his
group at work that had resulted in solving other cases.
He was about to elucidate this kit-and-run cases when
his death came in a flash.

I am the one who was directly involved in
identifying and catching the killer. How did the events
unfold?

I was home after a day of work that seemed quiet,
when the officer on duty announced to me by phone:

"I don't know how to report you, but something
terrible happened."

"What happened ? Is something burning?" I answered him with a question.

"No! ... boss ... an acquaintance of mine called me ... (I can tell you it's a source)." The officer's voice was interrupted, betraying the emotion that prevailed on him.

"Say it once, what happened?"

"Well ... he told me that Lieutenant Wise was killed in a bar ..."

"In a bar?" I asked him.

"Yes, at a bar located at the bus station in District D."

" The one in O. Street?"

"Yes boss, he answered. This source that I told you about (continued the officer) told me that it was a brawl among consumers and that in the end, Wise was killed."

"This source of yours", I asked him, "was it there too? When did all this happen?"

" I think 10 minutes ago", the officer explained to me.

When the telephone conversation was over, I ordered him to send the research team to the scene, the team on duty according to the planning and to report on the events, informing him that I was leaving right at that moment to the scene.

I got out of the block where I lived, I got into the car I had left in the parking lot and less than 10 minutes, I arrived. There, on the sidewalk, Lieutenant Wise was lying face up, wearing civilian clothes.

I leaned over him and I noticed he had no pulse, his body was still warm, and the shirt under his coat, was soaked in blood over his heart. Near the corpse there was a burning tea light candle. I looked around, but there was no one.

I headed to the bar at the bus station, but inside there were only the bartender and two men standing next to the counter. After I told them who I was, the bartender told me he did not know how it happened, only that the two men knew details about the case.

The two told me one by one, excited and without coordinating their explanations that it all started when a resident in the area entered the bar with a knife in his hand, saying he would kill everyone because he knew that his wife had cheated on him with each of the men there. One of the drinkers at the tables shouted to him:

"Go home! You're drunk, don't you see?"

When the attacker rushed to them, they defended themselves with chairs, screaming and swearing at him. But he gave up, saying:

"Nevermind! I'm gonna get back home and find out from my whore of a wife with whom she was … or I kill her.

The two men in the bar continued telling me that at that moment Lieutenant Wise also appeared at the door, who sought to calm things down.

The aggressor and the officer had a dialogue and it resulted that the former had given up his killer ideas. When he was about to get out of the bar, the aggressor turned around in a flash and stabbed him in the chest.

"This is because you are one of those who slept with her,too!" the murderer screamed, while the lieutenant collapsed to the ground.

As I was interrogating the three, I saw that a lot of curious people, older clients of the bar, but also many children, had gathered around the bar. Among the latter, a child addresses me by screaming:

"We know him, we know who he is, he lives in our block."

I wanted to call the one who had told me the piece of information and bring him to me, but Sergeant Brown, the law enforcement agent, equipped with munition, rubber cane, belt and handcuffs emerged from the crowd surrounding him.

I asked him what he was doing there and he told me he was on duty in the market area and that he heard the rumor about what happened.

He told me that from the discussions he had with a few people (whom he got to know while being on duty in that neighborhood for many years), he knew who the criminal was. He reported to me:

"If you allow me, I'll go and shoot him." The dialogue we had in front of the crowd seemed unnatural.

"Why shoot him? Go and arrest him!"

" I'll shoot him, you know! Because he killed the Lieutenant."

"Hey, man, it's not you who should do justice", I shouted. "Do you want to go to prison?"

"But, boss, he killed someone!"here with me, the team is coming now."

"I'm going to arrest him," he continued, "and if he doesn't abide, I'll shoot him."

"You'll shoot him if he doesn't stop after you fire a warning shot."

The NCO ran away followed by a mob of young people and children. He stopped at one point, turned nervously to those who followed him, shouting:

"Stay here, he's dangerous!"

But the threat was in vain, because they continued to pursue him.

Remaining at the scene, I interrogated a few men, who said they knew the victim, they were his neighbors.

They were trying to understand how some advice coming from a man with good intentions ended tragically.

Suddenly, a howling noise of human voices with screams and swearing, could be heard from the area in which the NCO had left, and afterward the crowd appeared, headed by the NCO, with the gun in one hand, and with the other pushing a handcuffed man.

It was a scene resembling an ancient tragedy: the body of the lieutenant lying on the sidewalk at the end of which there was the one who killed him, the NCO with the gun in his hand, crying and telling me!

"He didn't run chief! He stopped when I ordered him,

No one had come from the headquarters yet.

I asked the driver of a car in the parking lot to drive the NCO and the arrested person in handcuffs. I ordered Sergeant Brown to go to the headquarters and hand him over to the police unit.

When Brown came out of the parking lot, then a team made up of the officers of the Judicial Department also arrived. The investigations were taken over by a team led by a criminal prosecutor.

I never knew who was in charge of finalizing this case. I was convinced that I would be called, at least for the on-site research report.

Although it was I who had performed the first procedural activities, no one told me anything. Instead, I made sure I congratulated sergeant Brown and awarded him for the thorough way he did his job.

I keep wondering why did Lieutenant Wise die? Because he wanted to be an honorable citizen of the community or because he was a policeman? He died at the beginning of his career and I did not hear anyone among the young officers working in this city talk about him. I appreciate him even after his death.

***

THE "BUST" CASE

THE "BUST" CASE

Many times, in my memories, I compare the work of investigating crimes with that of a surgeon. I participated a few times in the operating room , due to my specialty in forensics and I found that a surgeon, even if well-prepared, he can get his job done only with a team of doctors who help him in his activities. It's the anesthesiologists I am talking about, the doctor considered to be the "second hand" and the average staff without whom there is no achievement.

It is the same with criminal investigations starting from the on-site investigation and ending with drafting reports. I am thinking about the "BUST" case, known in judicial practice since the 80s of the last century. A group of officers endeavored to solve one of the hardest murder cases. A road test site for driver schools was arranged on the western side of the cemetery. Here, for obtaining the driving license.

The test site was very crowded; the candidates were quiet until they entered the test site. For a nature call, there was no particular place. The participants, when they had such needs, penetrated the cemetery through a hole in its wall, relieving themselves in the cemetery bushes.

One of the students discovered a paper bag on a tomb whose soil had been compressed. He wanted to break a piece of it to use it as toilet paper, but found another canvas bag in it. When he overturned it, terrified, he saw that it was the trunk of a human body, armless, eviscerated, and some remains of cotton fabric could be seen in the thoracic cavity.

When I arrived at the scene, a multitude of future drivers were gathered around the hole in the cemetery wall. I found that the fragment in the corpse did not show any bleeding of the cut tissues, proving that the parts had been detached postmortem.

It was part of a man's body that the forensic doctor examined and indicated that the person's age was between 25-30 years. According to our knowledge, the piece of fabric inside the chest, on the spot where the internal organs had been removed, came from a cotton body shirt. On the right side, near the collar, there was a tear-shaped like an L, which had its edges sewn with thick beige thread; this bust was found wrapped in a pillowcase.

I considered then, that it was one of the cases that one would find in beds in hospitals or boarding schools. They used to be all placed into multi-layer paper bags. According to its appearance, the bag was new, it hadn't been used. We all concluded that such bags were for sale in shops.

On its surface, somewhere above the logo, there was a group of figures placed on two rows, it was a mathematical subtraction. Looking at the figures of the subtraction, I found that the one who had solved it made a mistake, the result being greater by a few units than the real one. There were no other traces of forensic value in the place where the bag was found. Starting from the result of the on-site research, each of the team members did specific activities to their specialization.

The forensic doctor took the bust to the forensic laboratory inside the hospital to examine its dissection in detail. The prosecutor and two officers prepared and trained all the policemen in the field. I took the paper bag, the pillowcase and the body shirt. I remember laying them in a room, on the floor and letting them dry. The next day, I examined these items with a binocular microscope in the light of a strong reflector.

I discovered on them flower seeds, wooden fragments (splinters), small leaves of plants I did not know, as well as white and black cat hairs. From the paper bag I took as evidence, by shooting, the writing in the form of figures as well as the typed text that was part of the logo. These were used to find out where exactly in the city area, quantities of bags had been distributed for sale. Subsequent checks established that an amount of these bags were sold in several profile stores in the area.

The woman who had sold that specific bag was found. She said she remembered the buyer as a medium-sized man, but that she was not the one who wrote the figures on the bag. Almost without realizing the ridiculous situation, she said: "I can't be the one who wrote because I know how to do subtractions correctly."

For almost two months, checks were made to establish any cases of missing people.

At the same time, I examined the thread with which the L-shaped rupture was sewn and I established that it was a beige macrame thread made up of three strands twisted to the right. There were not many cases of missing people, and with the investigation neither of them led to the identification of the one who was killed. Usually when investigations aren't going anywhere, energies and concerns decrease in intensity; but in that case it was not so, because a young man who had not come home to his parents for several months was reported missing.

The person in question worked in a warehouse of building materials, the last time he was at his parent's house on the occasion of the winter holidays, and lived near his workplace, in a bachelor apartment.

When I got to the home of the missing person's parents, I found that they had two cats: a white one and a black one, and in a kitchen table drawer I found a small roll of macrame thread. The evidence and clues we had that far were not sufficient to solve the case and we had to search the house of the alleged victim, too.

The administrator of the block told the police that the one in question was among the violent tenants, which is why none of the people staying there wanted to share the room with him. He only knew that the guy had been missing for a few months from his dwelling, but he didn't venture to find out why. Since then, he said, it had been quiet in the block. Only one tenant was getting on well with him, he was called George, a short man, a bit deaf and wicked, but he hadn't not been seen around either.

When the administrator was asked to accompany us to the room where the two lived, he showed undisguised fear, saying that it would be best to go there without him.

"He scared many people and I am afraid, I do not know what he might do if we find him in the room," said the administrator.

What I found in the room was unimaginable. Apart from the disorder and mess that dominated the whole room, I found that one of the beds had a shriveled mattress, having been soaked with a strong substance, the linoleum below it had a thick, cracked layer that I sensed was blood.

On the wall above the bed there was a large brown-reddish stain, with many splashes of the same color, it was partially covered with a 50/80 cm paper print that represented, as written at the bottom, a carpet. The administrator could not give any explanations. All kinds of dirty clothing were scattered on the other bed, proving that no one had been sleeping there.

I noticed the pillow on that bed, covered was dressed in a pillowcase similar to the one in which the bust had been found in the cemetery. Where were the two people living there? No one could give any hint. The research we did were to no avail, too.

Later, the non-commissioned officers who were on duty in the central market managed to identify and detain George. The one who handled his hearing and investigation told me that the hearing was relatively easy, he immediately admitted that he had killed Sean. This is what he said about the way he had killed the man: "When we came back from work, we established to cook together.

Sean was in charge of the food. He had brought cornflour, sausages, pork and a demijohn of wine from home. We cooked together, we ate, drank and we started to quarrel. He told me that I was deaf and stupid, and I told him he was so wimpy and filthy. We started a fight, but he was stronger, he squeezed my head and my throat under his armpit. He sat on the bed, squeezing my head; with his left arm he was hitting my head with a welding pipe.

I was screaming, shouting and I couldn't get rid of the grip but because I was near the table (where I knew there was a knife) I struggled, gropping, I grabbed the knife and with my last strength I stabbed him several times in his stomach. When he weakened the grip, he fell hitting his head against the wall and then, I hit him in the head with his welding pipe. I left him on his bed, and I fell on my bed. When I woke up in the morning, Sean was dead face up, all his blood had been flowing on the mattress and the linoleum under the bed.

For a few days I cut him into pieces, first his insides and then the head, I put them in plastic bags and during the night, I threw them in the water. I did the same with his feet. I put his hands in a plastic bag and took them into the yard of a relative of mine, where I threw them in the outdoor toilet. For the thorax it was harder; I had to buy a paper bag but the seller from the bookstore told me to buy a picture carpet, too.

I took them, I put the bust in the bag, and after I had wrapped it in the pillowcase, I glued the carpet picture on the wall above the bed to hide the blood stains and with the bag under my armpit I set off to the tram station in order to dump it into my relative's yard toilet.

I did not get there because there was a blackout and the tram stopped next to the cemetery. The blackout lasted a long time, the tram was not leaving and I decided to go off. In the darkness of the night I went to the cemetery, where I threw it on a tomb. I thought I would get away with it, " said George.

As the investigation could not be closed only with the murderer's confession, it was decided, and when they were washed throwing two buckets of water over them, the letters S and D tattooed in blue ink appeared on the left forearm, and there was the proof they were S.D.'s arms.

As we were leaving the place a lot of people shouted: prosecutors, people like these must be sentenced to death!

It was not the way the crowd wanted, the judges sentenced him to prison which he executed without creating problems and he was released on parole.

***

08

THE CHEMICAL TRAP

THE CHEMICAL TRAP

On the road that crosses over the bridge from S. to B., right after the forested dam, you encounter, on the right, the buildings of a slaughterhouse.

I was only once in this slaughterhouse to identify and catch a meat thief that seemed straight out of a sci-fi movie.

The director of this slaughterhouse, engineer Cole, told me the following when I arrived in his office: "The building of this animal slaughter unit and manufacture of meat products has a slaughter line, a storage room for the semi-frozen meat as well as sectors for the preparation of meat products.

The location was chosen to take into account its closeness to the water, relatively far from the rural and urban settlements, using as raw material the animals in the zootechnical units in the area.

We regularly deliver pork and beef carcasses for both the local and export market, having contracts with several countries. According to the contract, the job was going quite well, until it was found that someone was stealing different amounts of meat from the few dozen refrigeration rooms.

When they would open the doors of the rooms where the sacrificed animals were stored, they would find that in some of them, someone had cut pieces of muscle.

The representatives of the external clients had also faced this situation several times, and they refused the reception of several tens of tons of meat."

"Do you realize?" the director continued, "we were the ones who had to deal with the incurred losses, we are one step away from closing everything."

I called you, the director told me, because you were recommended as the expert who can catch those producing this damage."

I had to find those thieves but I had to see if the slaughterhouse was the right place to use one of the forensic methods known as the chemical trap. The method is very effective, it's a kind of weapon used to hunt down the "pray".

But the weapon is not as important as the skill of the one who knows how to use it. To cumulatively succeed, the following conditions must be fulfilled: the crime must be repeatedly committed in the same place, the suspects must be part of the closed group of those who have access to the place where the assets are stolen from, non -hazardous and non-accessible substances must be used and not the least, the secret of what is going on must be kept.

For these reasons, I went to the slaughterhouse. I was impressed by the cleverness of how everything was organized there: cleanliness, order and especially the design of the technological lines.

A long hall coming from the slaughter area was connected to several dozen refrigerated rooms, each with a lined door with insulating material fixed on rollers, sliding easily for both closing and opening.

All along the ceiling of the hall, there was a ditch with metal edges in which metal hooks were sliding fastened two by two at the ends of a metal bar.

Half of a pork carcass was hanging on each hook. These hooks were inserted through the ceiling ditch into the refrigerated rooms.

The same channels with metal edges were arranged parallel to a distance of about 60-70 m from each other on the ceiling of each room.

Here was where the aforementioned carcasses would be stored until they were delivered to the beneficiaries, loaded into trucks that were towing refrigeration containers.

The carcasses of the sacrificed animals looked like pictures taken from "Rocky", the Silvester Stallone movie, where the hero used such carcasses as training bags.

"You see, these doors are closed by a committee, seals are placed on them and a report is written by the committee. After the meat has been placed inside, the temperature is checked. As you can see, there is a thermometer here that indicates the indoor temperature.

The technicians on duty pass on this hall permanently, checking the integrity of the locks and the temperature.

Under these conditions, several times, when the doors were opened and we wanted to load the goods in the isotherms of the ramp, we were astonished to find the chopped carcasses and the lack of small quantities of them.

The only way to enter here is through the doors you see. The locks were always intact. The refrigerated rooms have bulkheads, the floor and the ceiling are the same, thermally insulated.

We cannot explain how such a phenomenon happens, that otherwise I cannot call it," the director P. ended.

I entered one of these rooms and found that what he had told me was true. There were no releases in the walls or ceiling, instead I found that a parallelepiped made of galvanized steel with a width of about 1 m and a depth of 50 cm was going down from the ceiling, on the side walls.

The bottom of the parallelepiped ended with an opening of the same dimensions at about 70 cm above the floor.

I asked what was the purpose of those hoses and I was told that they were spaces through which the cold air circulated from the refrigerated installations located on the floor above the storage rooms.

I was explained that the refrigeration system was built like that from the beginning. I asked to go up there to see what it was about.

There, we found several rooms arranged one at the level of every two of the refrigeration rooms below. A deafening noise of electric engines came from inside them, engines with powerful propellers with many blades, protected by metal nets. The air current there was strong and cold. I asked the director if he could stop one of the fans.

He called the technician on duty, asking him to stop one of the fans. The technician protested for starters, motivating that the installation can be broken, but in the end, one of the fans was stopped.

Followed by the director and the technician, I entered one of these rooms that was actually a huge refrigerator.

This "refrigerator" generated the cold air due to the compression of a gas passing through a thick coil, pushing the cold air brought by the fan's blades from outside and reaching the room below where the carcasses were stored.

With all the objections of those who accompanied me, using a flashlight, I passed through the fan's blades and looked down through the parallelepiped, finding that the galvanized steel was fixed on an edge iron skeleton, which had the shape of a staircase, where a medium -sized person could climb and descend easily.

When I returned to the director's office, I explained my hypothesis, which was based on my findings.

I told them that in my opinion, the author was part of the security staff who supervised the proper functioning of the refrigeration system. Both the director and the technician were skeptical.

"How do you think you can catch this bastard who does more damage than stealing?" I replied that I could do it using a forensic trap.

"I assume you do not refer to that metal machine that catches the paws of the prey animals? " one of the engineers who participated in our discussion asked me.

"I will explain tomorrow when I come back with the substance I will use." The collective confusion was even greater.

"What do you mean ... do you want to use a chemical substance?" the same engineer asked me, puzzled.

I didn't explain anything to them that day. I returned the next day after I had prepared a pure grease cream in which I mixed a few grams of BON acid-this substance that I had in a small quantity, being given by the Forensics Institute precisely for this kind of activity.

It is used in the paint industry as an additive, causing the paint to withstand both textile and leather goods.

This yellow-green dust with strong fluorescence sticks to the hands and clothing of a suspect when he touches the places where the substance is applied. From my previous experiments, I found that BON acid sticks to human skin and cannot be wiped, washed or cleaned for 14 days from contact.

When embedded in a thin layer of pure grease, in the light of day it is imperceptible. Its presence is immediately noticeable under the incidence of ultraviolet rays.

When I returned to the slaughterhouse, in the presence of those who were unbelieving, I entered the hoses of six refrigeration rooms picked randomly, and with a brush I applied a consistent layer from the box with my preparation on the edge iron steps. I did this for the lower steps of the parallelepiped.

When I finished, we prepared a report, mentioning what we have done, we all signed and decided to proceed as follows:

"We shall keep the secret of our actions."

"We'll continue to store meat in those rooms, waiting for the moment when we find again that meat is missing."

They continued to be skeptical. It had been almost three weeks, when, on a Saturday, while I was with all my colleagues at the shooting range for training, the shooting was interrupted because from the high edge of the range I was calling for:

"Tomassi , come on the slaughterhouse quickly, they stole meat again."

I replied to him from the waiting line, where I was waiting to shoot, that we shouldn't hurry.

"Come on Tomassi, everyone is waiting for you, especially the director …"

I explained to the officer that it was ok it happened. What we were going to do would take at least two days. When I arrived again at the slaughterhouse, I asked them to draw up a list of all the people who were on duty at the time they found the theft and in the previous days.

All that had to be done was to record all the staff, because as they were working in shifts, all of them could be potential thieves.

And as I had foreseen, checking the presence of BON acid on the bodies of the suspects was performed on Monday morning. Six men who were suspects.

I asked each one to come to the office where I had the UV lamp, but only after they washed their hands well at the sinks in an adjacent room.

Confused, when I lit the UV lamp, they stretched their shaking hands palms up, to check the presence of yellow-green fluorescence, specific to the BON acid.

The result was negative. I let them leave and told them that the closed circle of suspects were not included all those who had been on duty during the critical period.

We looked at each other in silence and the only one who expressed his opinion was an employee (the one who had been in charge of calling the suspects) who said:

"One is missing. I will check why he hasn't come."

The situation was solved by one of the engineers, who brought the missing one to the workplace. When he entered the room he said he would not wash his hands, he knew what it was about and that it was only then that he stole meat. His short confession without anyone asking him was clear proof that he was the author. However, those present insisted on his hands being examined under the UV light. The yellow-green fluorescence was on both palms but not only there, it was on his face,too.

The fluorescence, persisted on his hands and face after being wiped with a towel. No one told him anything and the investigation later followed its course.

I only remember the director of the slaughterhouse telling me on departure that he did not initially believe that it all went as I had assumed.

"A bastard, he did more harm to us than the value of the meat he stole. That's people ! I was a paternal leader, helping many of my employees to solve their family problems," director Cole said bitterly.

Although my effort was not in vain, the director did not want the author to be sent to court, asking the officer to conclude the investigations and giving up the complaint.

For me, the director's behavior was not a surprise. According to the features of his face, according the way he spoke, I sensed a generous man, a noble character.

***

09 GALTON'S LINE VS AFIS

GALTON'S LINE VS AFIS

In the judicial-criminal practice there are many files in which the identification of the bad guys and their conviction is based on the digital trail left by them in the area of the crime. Few know that to get here, the sharp mind of some English scientists and the successful practice of police officers in a country in Latin America was needed.

The fathers of Dactyloscopy (this is the branch of forensics focused on studying fingerprints) are three English men, all living during the Victorian era, starting with Herchel, Faulds and ending with Francis Galton. The latter, a scientist concerned with several subjects (Charles Darwin's cousin) knowing about the research of the first two, conducted a thorough study on the fingerprints on people's fingers.

The scientist, leading his team, "harvested" for research the fingerprints of over 8000 people. He got the fingerprints from the people who visited the exhibitions that took place in High Park in London. The fingerprint was taken for a few penniers per person.

After several years, of examining the tens of thousands of fingerprints with a magnifying glass on feet (to which the dactyloscopy experts added a glass reticle, and on its diameter he drew a line) the scientist publishes his conclusions in 1892, in a book entitled "Fingerprint".

The author concluded that the papillary ridges created by the fingers of each person are unique and certainly lead to the person's identification. Later he proposed to Scotland Yard this method of identifying criminals.

This is the act of birth of dactyloscopy. What Gaston established was not immediately applied. A policeman from South America, Vucetich, had to solve the famous case Francesca Rojas based on the exploitation of finger blood traces taken from the scene in the case of the murder of two boys.

He made his success public, saying it was the result of reading the book "Fingerprint". At that time in France, and not only, the "French bertillonage " was " in power" the anthropometric model of criminal registration of the criminals.

Quickly, the use of fingerprints spread to the police sections in the South American and European states. Specifically, the basis of identification consists in comparing the characteristics of the traces left by the criminals at the scene of the crime to the characteristics of the model fingerprints got from the suspects.

The important moments of the identification process are three: the first, the revealing and lifting of the traces in the crime field, the second, the obtaining of the comparative model fingerprints and the third party, the comparative examination of the two categories of fingerprints, trace and comparative model. All three are important with the connection "sine qua non" between them.

However, the most important is the first, because without it, there is no identification.

Discovering the traces on the scene is the work of the "fieldworker" policemen around the world. They are the soldiers of the unseen war that the police and the whole criminal justice system win against crime. We can say they are the unknown heroes of this war. Their activity continues by comparing the traces to the impressions of the suspects.

I remember that in my years of study, the teachers would show and ask us to repeat daily the fingerprinting procedures from different media: glass, wood, paper, ceramics, plastic, etc.

In my first years of practical activity, I was quite well trained in this field. The instrument I used (which is still being used now) in the comparative examination is the magnifying glass on feet, with a reticle, the famous line bearing Galton's name.

The problem that arises every time after picking up the traces of the crime field is that of the closed circle of suspects. Who should establish this circle? It would be natural to have it done by the police in the operative teams. To establish these circles, police around the world have created dactyloscopy records of former criminals.

These records are known as criminal records. The special forensic records are the decadactylation and monodactylation on criteria inherited from Galton or German dactyloscopy experts. The redoubtable "weapon" for these records remains Galton's magnifying glass. The only obstacle is the enormous quantity of impressions from the records known as the catalogs, which are several thousand in number.

A dactyloscopy expert can perform several hundred comparisons per day.

The happiest case is when there are only a few people in the circle of suspects and for this it is necessary to do detailed investigations through on-site research, otherwise the investigated offenses remain with unknown authors.

For me, my first case in the practice of forensics was a success in the field of dactyloscopy. It gives me pleasure to tell that story even now.

In the fall of 1985, I was working at the Forensics Laboratory within the S. City Police Department. I was asked to carry out the on-site investigation for a burglary, committed at a grocery store, near the train station.

I was teaming up with an officer from the judicial department who asked me if I had done investigations on the scene; I told him no, but added I was good at it, because in school I had done countless such practical activities. What followed was exactly like in the school laboratories.

The entrance door of the store, facing the street, was intact. Behind the building of the grocery store, there was a window with broken glass, and the glass pieces were placed upright, against the wall.

When I examined them in transparency, I found that on their surface there were finger traces of sebum for all five fingers on one hand, four on one part and one on the other part.

The metal bars of the window were made of steel strips, cut in four places and bent inward. There were iron filling, broken glass and two pieces of a hacksaw blade on the window sill.

There was quite a large hole created in the bar, and in the cut rough sides of the metal plates there were green cloth lints.

It felt like we were during the dactyloscopy laboratory classes at the police school. At the end of the research, when I was preparing the report, Officer Jenkins told me: "You're good at it, Tomassi."

In the laboratory, while photographing the finger traces on the glass, I was called to the Deputy Chief of Police in S. City. He asked me to report what I had done on-site. I told him what I had done, showing him the traces I had picked up from the place.

The boss looked at them and asked me what I would do next. I reported that I would make the photographic plate, I would pack the traces and I would hand them to my superior officer.

"Anything else?"

I replied that my job was over there.

"And when are you going to do the dactyloscopy comparisons with the impressions of the suspects?"

"When Officer Jenkins makes them available to me."

"But you, there, at the grocery store, haven't you established who the suspects are?"

"No! Because I came to the laboratory to end what I've started on site, the judicial officer being the one to establish the circle of suspects."

"My dear, as it is your first case, let me show you how to do it! I mean that at the investigation on-site you must always execute all activities, not only forensic ones, to identify the criminal, not interrupting the investigation and research activity.

Here's how we will proceed !! The green cloth lines probably come from the criminal who entered through the cut bars. Do you agree with me that it comes from a military uniform?

I accepted that it was right, but where to find the military? Like a teacher, my boss continued his reasoning which proved to be flawless.

"The grocery store is near the train station and one of the travelers on the platform, probably a military man, may have committed the theft."

After that, he dialed a phone number and spoke to an unseen interlocutor, telling him:

"Check, who of your agents was on duty on the train station platform yesterday night? See what people he has identified and tell me the result."

After hanging up, he addressed me, clarifying:

"You can't know that the law enforcement agents should have the obligation to record in their service notebooks the identification data of the identified people.

I was waiting for the result of checking the NCO's notebook, the one who was on duty last night on the station's platform. My activity unfolded by the book. Indeed, in the non-commissioned officer's notebook the name of a soldier was found; he had come with a night train, to take a new train, where he lived.

The boss told me that the soldier was to be brought by the NCO who identified him and I had to make comparisons with his digital impressions. Towards the evening, the soldier was brought, I took his fingerprints, made the comparisons and found that the on-site traces, all five, were made by his left hand. Before reporting the result to my boss, I called Officer Jenkins, informing him of the present situation.

I waited for him and together we went to report the result. The boss was a little troubled by the presence of Officer Jenkins, but I reported that I had notified him.

"Nice of you! But Jenkins had to do what I did. I did it for you because it is your first case."

I thanked him for the lesson he taught me and I confess that since then and until I retired, I acted in the same way in all the cases I was involved.

I was appreciated by many colleagues for my manner to proceed, as my former boss had taught me.

My result in the reported case was possible because I had a suspect, but not the same thing happened in the situation of money theft from a mine cash register. The trace we picked up there was impeccably clear.

I had revealed it with fluorescent yellow pigment on the circular latch of the cash register from where the money was stolen. The cashier stated that the register had no key and the door could be easily opened.

The research was not easy and the circle of suspects not be established immediately. It was considered that the authors are among the workers in the mine, which is why a few thousand people were fingerprinted. Until I left the Police Department of S. city there was no identification of the one who made the trace. After four decades, being retired, I learned that the file was classified as a lapse, the authors not being identified.

In 1990, I made an exchange jobs with the chief criminal officer from G. Here, in the first case I attended in tandem with a colleague from the judicial department, I picked up from the site the finger traces created on painted glass.

In this case it was about a police section office, where unknown authors forced the office door, stealing a copy of a contravention report.

The case seemed unusual. Such theft was not known in our experience. The police chiefs back then asked for investigations. When I asked for a suspect, the following were reported to me:

"It is a black, bearded sailor, who caused a scandal at the bar in the basement of the Orhideea hotel, breaking bottles and glasses. At the request of the staff in the bar, we went to the scene, a contravention report was written and he was given a copy, the duplicate being kept by the officer.

The officer arrived at the station, locked the documents, closed the door and left.

This morning the break-in was detected. The policeman remembered there was a sailor on a Liberian ship at anchor in the port. I wrote down the name on my agenda.

"Let's go get the sailor fingerprinted!" I said.

"Leave the sailor!" my colleague responded. "We have other cases."

I did not agree with him and we left all three to the Harbourmaster's Office. I got on board the ship accompanied by the representative of the Harbourmaster's Office.

Through the interpreter I asked the captain of the ship to bring the offender. When I was fingerprinting him, the policeman who had prepared the report whispered to my ear that he did not think this was the sailor in question because this one had no beard.

I clarified things immediately when, performing the dactyloscopy comparisons, I established that the traces were made by the fingers of his right hand. Subsequent investigations established that he had stolen the duplicate of the report in order not to notify the company that hired him as a sailor, about the crime he committed.

This case is another example from my experience as a dactyloscopy expert, but at the same time, the demonstration of the lasting things I learned from my mentor. The success was also because there was only one person in the circle of suspects. If the circle had been made up of several people, I doubt the result would have been positive.

Therefore, at present, the decadactyl and monodactyl record-keeping system is used. It is called Automated Fingerprint Identification System (AFIS) and this system has in its electronic memory the images of the finger impressions of all people in the police operative records.

The computer has a program that examines the finger traces on site in natural size in comparison with all the monodactylic impressions from the system records. The computer program of this system is based on the comparative analysis of the traces with the image of the monodactylic impressions recorded.

This identification is made based on the coincidence of the placement and the number of start points and end points of papillary ridges between the two images. Due to its program, the computer detects in a very short time all the impressions similar to the trace.

The dactyloscopy operators of the AFIS system have stated that if the dinger impressions of the suspect are in the data record, identification is certain.

The certification of the positive result is done by the dactyloscopy expert. For this, he draws up a report of dactyloscopic expertise. Although AFIS is the basis, the expert uses for his certainty, the same Galton's magnifying glass, a linear reticle.

In the practice of forensic expertise, but especially of dactyloscopy, a separation happened in the sense that the first category of forensics is those in the field, who are meant to investigate the site of the crime and to pick up the traces; and the second category is that of the laboratory operators, who didn't get to do on-site research.

Those in the first category work under all conditions, no matter whether it is cold, hot, night, a holiday, or a regular day and they go to less pleasant places of scents and images.

Those in the second category operate in pleasant, warm environments when it is cold, they have air conditioning when it is hot outside, and oftentimes they listen to Vivaldi or relaxation music.

The former ones are real astronauts dressed in all kinds of coverall suits, the latter work in white or blue robes and light footwear and have steaming coffee on the desk.

As I said above in the chain of the dactyloscopic identification activity, the main role is played by the typical forensics on the site; the success depends on the result of their work result. Many of them have Galton's magnifying glass as a precious item, as it is the basis of all computer programs, which are focused on the dactyloscopic identification of the person.

***

10 TREBLE CLEF

TREBLE CLEF

Traceological expertise has one of the dearest places in my memories. I was pleased to do such expertises because each case has its novelty, referring to identifying objects that have left traces during crimes.

In traceology, traces can be either "a shape" (representing the outer shape of the object that made it), "matter" (fragments of the physical bodies used by the criminals) or "striations" (those created by the hard bodies that have slipped on various surfaces), all leading to the identification of the object that created it, which in one way or another, are related to a criminal case.

I remember, from the multitude of cases I was asked to solve, different objects that were related to the crimes, such as: knives, sticks, axes, shoes, boots, car tires, animal hooves, sled runners, pliers, etc.

In one case, an object was shaped like an important graphic element for musical theory, that is the sol key. How was the sol key connected to an object involved in a murder, you will find out in the next lines.

The sol key is made of a spiral to the right linked to an upper loop and a descending line with a curved end, placed under the staff.

It has a beautiful, pleasant look, similar to the neck of a swan that is consonant with the beauty of the art bearing the name of music.

In the craftwork practice, we have seen some creations of ironmongery representing a flower pot holder that has a sol key as a hangpoint, made of different materials: iron, brass, plastic, etc.

On one of the cold mornings of winter, on the so-called green space in front of a ten-story block, the tenants who were going to work, discovered the body of a young woman, lying on the ground.

The investigations showed that the dead body scantily clad had been brought to that place; the traces on the ground to prove that the murder had been committed there were missing. At the necropsy they found that death was due to mechanical asphyxia caused by strangulation.

The face of the corpse had signs of swelling made by hitting with hard objects in the shape of fingers and the lips had ecchymoses caused by the same mechanism.

On the back of the victim, in the kidney area, the body had an ecchymosis shaped like the sol key. All these elements showed that before being abandoned in the place where she was found, the victim was undressed and by pressing on her body a sol key shape, the ecchymosis was formed.

At the end of the on-site research and the forensic expertise it was concluded that it was a murder case with a body of unknown identity. Subsequent research and investigations were difficult and did not lead to any results.

The suspect could have been anyone in the neighborhood where the body had been found. The number of people living in the neighborhood exceeded by far the number of a medium-sized city. When the investigations seemed to go nowhere, an anonymous phone addressed to the police dispatcher indicated an apartment in the block, in front of which the corpse was found.

The search conducted at the indicated apartment revealed that it belonged to an unemployed man, who was doing regular car transport to bring for trade various products such as: chewing gum, jeans, underwear, etc.

He was not found at home for a long time. Searching the apartment, the investigators found in one of the rooms on the floor a brass flower holder that had a wrought iron hanger in the shape of the sol key.

The traceological expertise performed on the trace of the victim's body proved that was the object which created the sign.

The owner of the apartment said he did not know anything about it, having no connection with the body found in front of the block.

He also stated that he had a friend to whom he gave the key to his apartment for money, where he probably had love encounters with different women. The friend was the owner of a small shop, where goods brought by different people were sold.

The owner of the store did not want to admit anything, although the other seller acknowledged that the dead woman was her colleague. Hardly, the one in question, facing the evidence, admitted that he did not want to kill his employee.

The deed was committed as follows: he proposed to his employee in question to have sexual intercourse with him, but she strongly refused. To fulfill his desire, after some time, he asked the employee to go to his home to do some cleaning, indicating the place where the apartment was.

The woman, not taking into account the danger she was exposed to, accepted, going to the indicated neighborhood and began to clean the apartment.

While cleaning, the employer arrived to check how the apartment was being cleaned. Then he proposed to the woman to have sex. Because she refused him, he became violent, stripping her and as he was fighting with her, they fell on the floor. He failed to fulfill his desire because of the violent opposition of the victim, which is why he slapped her several times, knocked her down to the floor and because she was screaming, he strangled her.

He thought she wouldn't die, but when she stopped screaming, he found that she wasn't breathing anymore. In order to get rid of the body, after he put a few clothes on her, he waited for the night and taking advantage of the silence in the block, he removed the body, holding her in his arms and abandoned her where she was found.

That is why he showed concern in front of the other seller about her colleague missing from work. He was sorry about what happened, considering it was both his and her fault. He had never thought that he would be identified with the help of a sol key shaped flower pot holder.

***

THE CASE THAT PUSHED ME AWAY FROM FORENSICS

THE CASE THAT PUSHED ME AWAY FROM FORENSICS

The story of this case began around 1982-1983, a few years after I had moved on request from the City Police A. to the one in city B.. My move was meant to get me closer to my family, to my parents.

At that time there was a campaign (otherwise justified) for solving the U.A.files (unknown authors) by exploiting as a priority the traces picked up from the on-site research in such cases.

It was a request made to the forensics, but the officers from the judicial department had the responsibility; they had the records of U.A. files and the forensics being asked to join them in this work. I knew that in the country and in other areas, forensics didn't use to strive to "exploit" the traces of the files with unidentified authors. In my city the situation was different and this was because the criminal investigation and forensics department had friendly co-operation, not imposed by the authority. A former class colleague from the police school, was in charge of " the homicide" line of action and had the Frances case. He informed me about the topic of this murder in the research of which he had not been involved from the beginning.

"Let's look in this file that's almost 10 years old! I have fingerprints and documentary evidence inside and yet it is not active."

"With fingerprints and documentary evidence!?"

"Yes! The Gordian knot, so to speak, there is a fingerprint trace revealed from a bottle of wine found on the table where the murder was committed, which was established to have been made by one of the victim's husband's fingers."

"Well, if so, what's the "Gordian knot"?"

"It is, because at the time the murder was committed, the husband was convicted and was executing a prison sentence. He was in prison; it was checked and established as a fact."

"As if it were a Sci-Fi movie! But what does the document refer to?"

"Look, I'll leave here all these files about the Frances case, read them to know what happened and what was done; I have other homicides with unknown authors "inherited" from officers who are now retirees. I was not present neither for the on-site investigation nor to that of the suspects."

Reading the procedural documents and the analyses in the case file, I understood that Frances lived on a street with poor hovels and she was a prostitute who had not been seen by the neighbors for several days. Those closest to her entered the house and felt the smell of a corpse and therefore announced the police. A team of officers from the judicial department arrived on site, the chief criminal investigator, all led by the prosecutor accompanied by the coroner.

Frances was found under her metallic bed, naked, full of blood and under her left armpit she had a cut wound. The objects were scattered in the room. On the table in the room (covered with paper from a paper bag) there were two glasses and a bottle, all empty. It was also found that on the "tablecloth" ie the paper bag, an illegible text was written with a pencil. The autopsy revealed that the victim died by being stabbed with a knife, that the author had pushed through the wound inside the chest; a knife that the coroner took out after removing the sternum of the corpse. The research that followed established that on the glasses and the bottle on the table there were some fragments of fingerprints out of which only one taken from the glass had eight-digit identification elements.

The text consisted of a few words out of which one could understand: "Who ... for ...... dollars". The words and graphic fragments were made in bold and included only the lower part of incomplete letters. The investigations carried out among the neighbors established that the victim earned her living from prostitution, and she would bring customers to her home. Her husband was in prison and lately, a former customer (and tenant) would come to Frances's house and ask for a debt of 50 dollars, which she could not pay because "she was poor, gentlemen!" as one of the neighbors stated. While reading the documents in the file, I reached a photographic sheet with a fingerprint picked up from the glass with the impression of the index finger of the victim's husband. Two sheets with the ten-digit impressions of the husband and the former customer asking Frances for money were attached to the sheet.

The criminal officer who had prepared the sheet indicated with arrows eight common characteristic elements between the trace and the control impression. I examined the demonstration made and found that, indeed the two papillary drawings shared the same corresponding elements.

The situation got even more bizarre when I read a few reports of the officers who conducted investigations about the former customer. It turned out that he was a drunkard, violent in the family and his entourage, without a stable job and who had stated, in front of his glassmates, that he had killed "Frances, the whore" because she did not want to pay her debt. Vexed by such a situation, I wanted to fingerprint the two suspects. I did this and what I had suspected proved to be true. The one who had fingerprinted the two suspects immediately after the on-site investigation, for an unknown reason, reversed the headings with the identity data, so that on the former client's sheet he wrote the husband's name and vice versa.

This situation had been laying unresolved for over 10 years and no one had done anything to solve it. I was pleased that I was the one who did it. My joy, which I shared with my colleagues, was immense. I had solved the mystery of the fingerprint that would have been created by the fingers of the husband who was in prison at the time the murder was committed. Now it was clear: the trace was made by the one who stated he had killed Frances. For this reason, I prepared a sort of draft, in which I explained my approach, a work that had not been asked for by anybody, procedurally speaking.

I showed it to the judicial department, the criminal prosecutor and the chief prosecutor. They all congratulated me, but at the same time they asked me, off-record, to see what can be done about the text written by the author on the "tablecloth" at the scene.

"You will not do anything!" my subordinate, a criminal investigator older than me, with real talent and skill in forensic expertise, cut me off.-?!

"As you know I like the judicial graphics, I tried to decipher that text and I think the scriptor wanted to write: "Whoever comes, should know I killed her for 50 dollars."

Next, the officer explained to me, showing the enlarged photo of the text:

"You see that the graphic path of each letter is interrupted in its upper part. The author of the text, either he was in a hurry or was in a state of nervous tension (he'd just killed a person) and the pencil (which I think was blunt) managed to make contact with the surface, i.e. the paper bag, only at the bottom of each letter. Because of this, the text seemed meaningless. I know and I think you know too, that the Latin alphabet writing movement is circular.

In the examinations made then, immediately after the on-site investigation, I appreciated that it was right to remake the missing path of each letter and I found that the text was legible and meaningful.

"Well, I burst, but why didn't you do this, I mean, this demonstration?"

"Why? For two reasons: firstly because my boss then, an arrogant, full of himself, did not ask me for this. He considered me a backward, not like him, a college graduate and the second reason ..."

How can I tell you, if others did not take responsibility for this case, why should I do it, the one from forensics?

"What do you mean?"

"Well, what to say? With the reconstructed text and model texts for comparison written by the author of the murder, I went to the central expertise laboratory."

"Right! And did you talk to the experts there?"

"I had gone to ask for an opinion from the best. After I told them who I was, I had gone there dressed in uniform, I told them about the case, I showed them the texts and I expressed my opinion. Do you know what they told me after examining the texts quite carefully?"

"??!"

"It's a great responsibility you're taking! Let the investigators establish the truth."

"So did they tell you?"

"Yes, they did so! And I tell you the same: let the judicial officers solve the case."

"But, this is a murder we're talking about, a human being was atrociously killed."

"It may be as you say, but as the chief coroner said...

"Well, what about him?"

"Frances was a bad seed. She hooked with the wrong people and she paid for it."

"This is the doctor's opinion, but do you approve of my dealing with demonstrating the identity of the author of the incriminated text?"

"I do, but be careful! ..."

I did not take into account my older colleague's warning. In my enthusiasm, I started to draw up a work that was meant to be a draft of a future forensic expertise report. I was the head of the Criminal Investigation Department, but at the same time a simple criminal investigator who, besides managing the activity, was also asked many times, to investigate a large and varied number of crimes, starting from burglaries, thefts, fatal hit-and-runs, fires, work accidents, suicides and ending with homicides.

For these reasons, I carried out the work on the identification of the author of the document in a few months. I wanted that in January or February of the following year, when all the heads of the criminal investigation offices in the country when were to be summoned for the annual analysis, to show my work to some colleagues to share their opinion. First of all, I was thinking about handwriting expertise because, about the fingerprinting issue, I was convinced that things were clear. The analysis we were summoned to took place in our former police school. The places, the classrooms, the sports fields, the kitchen and the laboratories had been changed, but they brought back memories about the school I graduated in the summer of 1975.

During a break, right in front of the classroom and study room of the 26th Criminal Investigations Class, I met our former teacher, who became head of department in the Criminal Investigation Institute. I considered him our mentor, especially related to dactyloscopy issues. Although I did not want to consult him about my works, in an impulse of sympathy and recognition of his competence, I asked him to look at the two "drafts" of expertise and to share his opinion.

He agreed, and I thanked him for that. He looked silently at each of the works, stayed longer on the graphic one and finally, after returning them to me, he told me:

"Tomassi, it's not as you say. It is better to stay out of this and let the investigations department identify the author.

Maybe I had to shut up and stay with my thoughts.

"The people at the Central Laboratory said the same thing."

"Well, see? These guys are smart. I advise you again: stay out of it!"

I told him I would do that. And I did so onward, although both the prosecutor and the criminal investigators kept asking me what I did at the meeting. It had been almost a month since my meeting with my mentor when, an officer from the Criminal Institute called me on the "short" phone, and asked me in a harsh tone to "go on and report" about the two works.

I replied to the officer that there was no work I had done. I was thinking that no one asked me to make the two expertises. And as I was then more mature, I wouldn't continue telling them that if they wanted to know what it was, I would ask the judicial office to send the U.A. (unknown author) file of the murder whose victim was Frances.

A few minutes after the conversation, I was called by the head of the police, who, in the same hard tone, ordered me to send the works required by the Institute with a report. I reported that I had no work. Other phone calls followed with the head of the Institute and hence a whole fuss solved with tact and skill by the deputy chief of police, who made things clear for me.

"Please, don't let things get more tense. This is about the stiffened egos of some chiefs from the administrative, not the forensic department. You will go to the Criminal Institute tomorrow morning with the two works and if they want to ask for explanations, give them explanations. What you did so far is fine. I support you but give them your works that you call "drafts" and not "the final works".

I agreed with him. The next day, at 9:30 am I was in the meeting room of the Criminal Institute, in front of a group of experts from the Institute and from the Capital City Police. Although they had not studied my "drafts" they asked me to explain to them what it was about. I asked them to study my works first and then accuse me, for both the dactyloscopic and the graphic one. After half an hour, without telling me anything, I was sent back to my city. Back home, it was ordered that I didn't get a refund for my journey.

There was a period of silence from my bosses in the capital city, as if nothing had happened. I was thinking that they were up to something. And indeed, that's how things happened. What followed demonstrated the wickedness and hypocrisy of a Machiavellian process.

After almost eight months, at the annual meeting of the criminal investigators, where all the heads of office were called, I was set up a real "trial".

They used to read the yearly activity report in front of the new management. At the presidium, there were two chiefs of the national police management team and all of us in the so-called festivity room, were sitting in the red upholstered chairs. The general report was being read. We were paying great attention to what was being read, but also the facial expressions of the two big bosses.

After mentioning the positive results of the experts within the Forensics Institute, almost without any connection with what had been read, what followed was referring strictly to me … "Only through the competent intervention of the Forensics Institute officers, a serious violation of the law that would have naturally led to a law error with dramatic consequences was prevented"… Here, the one who was reading took a break to breathe, enough for the entire audience to come out of the numbness that had been seizing them.

"It is the case, the speaker continued, of Captain Tomassi who, by supererogation, wishing to solve a murder case with unknown authors exceeded his competences of criminal investigation expert moving to the field of forensic psychology."

On hearing the allegations that were brought to me, I stood up so that the chiefs on the stand could see the guilty one. Everyone in the room was looking at me and probably waiting to see what would happen to me.

I didn't know how to react. I was standing and looking at those in the stand, being aware that my fate depended on the two. They tried to continue reading the report aloud, but one of the two bosses stretched forth his hand to him and interrupted him.

"You, young man, he addressed me, what do you have to say about what was stated?"

In the previous seconds I had prepared an answer and after I stuffed it down I reported in a tone that I meant to be respectful, but also to prove that I was confident.

"Sir, I understand that my future in the police force as a forensic expert depends on what I will report.

"Come on, report!" he encouraged me.

"In the concerned case, as a forensic expert, without being asked procedurally, I compared a text that the author of the murder wrote on the scene with model writing samples of the two suspects: the husband and a tenant. I concluded that the author of the text is the tenant. There are here in the room colleagues and former teachers of mine from whom I learned that in the field of forensic graphics, the higher the number of suspects, the higher the degree of error, decreasing when their number is lower. There were two suspects in that case and I stated that the author of the writing was the tenant.

But because things have come to this point, you being reported my so-called "supererogation" for which I have to pay, I say here, in front of everyone, "I was wrong", but at the same time I report that I am a hypocrite, because within myself, I know that I'm right. But I conclude by saying again "I was wrong".

"But this suspect, what does he say?"

"I didn't interrogate him, but in all the statements he says "Yes, I killed her".

"O.K., sit down!"

Then he addressed the top brass:

"If your people are striving, as I see that this young man has done and you discourage them, that's why you have so many unsolved murders!"

I sat down, breathless and my heart was beating fast. Around me, I could hear:

"You've won the fight!"

"Yes, the fight, but not the war" commented another one.

During the break that followed, one of the superiors in the Capital Police Department came down among us and threatened me by saying:

"You'll see that you are not right! I will send to your city a team of experts to get new writing samples and they will make a better documented report, free from psychological considerations.

This is how things happened with the Forensic Institute but when this happened, the Frances case was closed. Back to my city, I told to the prosecutors what had happened. The two listened to me and lived with me the emotions I had experienced and I still had at that point.

"Look what we will do! prosecutor Greene said eventually. The case is about to enter the limitation period. The author has always been in prison for various offences: thefts, bodily injury and hooliganism.

He was only free for a month or two, in some way he served his sentence, but if the gentlemen at the Institute are so upset about what you wanted to do, when they come there will be nothing to do. That's it!

And so it was: when they came after a few months, the object of the dispute had disappeared. For me, instead, it was the beginning of the separation from forensics, the passion of my life.

I gave up later in 1991 when the non-recognition of my merits for the Frances case determined me to make a clean break for good with the practical work of forensics investigator.

***

A JUDICIAL ERROR WITH HISTORICAL CONSEQUENCES

A JUDICIAL ERROR WITH HISTORICAL CONSEQUENCES

As I have stated on several occasions, as it is a recent science, almost 200 years old, forensics is often defined differently by theorists and those who practice it. Thus, Hans Gross called it the science of "state of facts" in the criminal trial. Others, without nominating them, say that it is the creator of the methods of discovering and investigating offenses and criminals.

A concern of the human mind that can be called science, must epistemologically answer three questions:

1. does it has a subject to study?
2. does it has its research methods of the subject?

3. does it have value judgments
    (theories) which can be checked
    by its own study methods?

No one so far has analyzed forensics in specialized works in the light of the three requirements. Our answer is affirmative, because it has a complex subject, made up of those changes in the environment caused by the offender's actions, changes that are called traces. Forensic studies these changes in order to identify the one who created them.

The study of these traces is done by its own methods, which it has created with methods borrowed from other sciences, adapted to its specificity. Of all the methods, the most important are: the experiment (hence the name of expertise of the expert's work) and the comparative examination.

The purpose of these activities is to IDENTIFY THE PERSON. Regarding its own ideas and theories, we will refer to two value judgments specific to this science. The first refers to the fact that a person or a phenomenon can be similar to others, but identical only to itself. The second value judgment is that under identical conditions, the people and tools used in committing crimes, cause identical changes (traces). These are the features of forensics, which is not just a job as I had the chance to hear from anonymous people.

One of the branches of forensics, similar to the others, but distinct from them, is forensic graphology. It is subject of study, a trace that is specific only to man, that is writing. Writing represents that change of the environment that man will voluntarily create on different materials: stone, wood, glass, ceramics, metal, etc., with different tools (quill pen, pencil, pen, feather pen, brush), signs called letters and figures, representing human ideas, memories, thoughts and activities, which he wants to make known to himself or his fellow citizens. Writing is the result of the movement willingly made by man, but which has specific features for each writer, due to the dynamic stereotype that is fixed almost unconsciously in the movement of the hand. When they start learning how to write, all children have very similar types of writing.

During the intellectual evolution of man, due to the desire to include as much data as possible, each person seeks to make as many letters as possible in a short period. For this reason, the physical effort made by the hand is to be smaller and the writing faster. By repetition, the dynamic stereotype is formed and the same words and letters always have the same features; they relate the shape of the letters, their sizes, their position on the lines, the connection between them, starting points or ending features.

Their arrangement, orientation, construction and many other features are due to the unconscious movement of the hand. This unconscious movement of the hand is the one that gives the foundation of person identification.

The criminal investigators who deal with the examination of the writing styles used in committing crimes are called graphoscopic experts. Their preparation is specific to this field, using at the beginning the separate examinations of the writing in question on the one hand, and of the model one for comparison on the other, got from the suspects. The categories of letters to compare are anonymous letters, counterfeit signatures and figures. Many of the criminal cases have been supported by handwriting forensic expertises worthy of praise made by experts in the proof of the truth.

However, I encountered situations when famous criminal investigators challenged the truthfulness of my forensic writing expertises: "Sir, a prominent criminal investigator told me, I can change my writing and signature in various ways, without anyone realizing it's only me and not other different people." I explained to my interlocutor that he had not been the subject of any criminal case to have his writing examined and that his opinion was subjective.

It is true that our dialogue was not taking place at a scientific session, but at a festive event celebration sprinkled with a lot of exotic drinks. Over time, on different occasions, in my discussions with lawyers, I would often hear such opinions. I didn't agree with them then and I don't agree with them now either.

In my activity as a criminal investigator, I carried out over 1000 forensic expertises, which aimed at identifying the authors of anonymous writings or counterfeit signatures. My expertises in this field were the evidential support in as many criminal files.

I wondered where this mistrust was coming from, especially since it existed in the community of people of law and not in the great mass of human communities. For me, the answer came from a material published in 2005. The explanation was the Dreyfus case.

The artillery officer Dreyfus, an officer in the Great General Staff of the French Army in the ninth decade of the 19th century, was unfairly convicted of betrayal, the entire probation being based on the handwriting forensic expertise done at the beginning by three experts and later a fourth one, the famous Alphons Bertillon.

The latter, although he was not qualified in the field (he was the creator of the criminal recording method called anthropometry) concluded in the handwriting expertise that the author of the documents transmitted to the military attaché of the German Embassy in Paris was Dreyfus.

Thanks to the writer Emile Zola, who published back then the famous article "J'accuse" in the newspaper "L'Aurore", we found out the truth. France was then divided into two camps: one that defended Dreyfus and the other, that blamed him, not based on judicial evidence, but on anti-semitic feelings.

The realities following the publication of Zola's article demonstrated the failure of the research, all based on the handwriting forensic expertise executed by Bertillon.

This one, although unprepared, continued to keep his conviction, although the true traitor, Ferdinand Elerhazy, testified that he was the one who had handed over the documents to the German military attaché. The experts in judicial graphics relevantly considered that Bellonon took into consideration in his expertise only the similar elements between the two categories of letters, without taking into account the different ones.

Subsequently, the great French criminal investigator, Edmond Locard rightly stated that when an expert finds inconsistencies between the two categories of evidence: incriminating and comparative model, which he cannot explain, they must be included in the expertise report. Unfortunately, this is the truth, the beginnings of forensic graphoscopy were marked by this famous error, which is the basis of its lack of credibility in the eyes of forensic workers.

Two comments are necessary: a linguistic one and a historical one. The former refers to the terms "graphoscopy and graphology". The difference between these is that graphoscopy aims to identify the person according to the writing, and the graphology, that of establishing the character traits of the one who wrote a text.

The latter observation, the historical one is related to the connection between the judicial error in the Dreyfus case and the beginnings of the organized movement for the creation of the modern State of Israel.

In 1891, Theodor Herzl, a correspondent of the Viennese newspaper "Neue Freic Press", comes to Paris and follows Dreyfus's process being shocked by the anti-semitic manifestations in France. In 1896, Theodor Herzl publishes in Vienna "Der Judeststat" (the State of the Jews) in which he proposes as a solution to solve the rise of anti-semitism in Europe (the so-called "Jewish problem") the establishment of a Jewish state on the ancient territory of its ancestors. In 1897 the [1]Zionist Organization is formed; the

---

[1] Sion is the ancient name of Jerusalem.

first *Zionist Congress, proclaiming their purpose to "establish" a house for the Jewish people in Palestine.

***

13

FORENSICS AND PHOTOGRAPHY

FORENSICS AND PHOTOGRAPHY

Now, at the end of my professional career in forensics, I can say that photography, for me, was like a "quill" for the writer. If there had been no quill, all literary works would have remained in the minds of the writers and would not have reached the sheets and been appreciated by people. The same with photography, if it had not existed, everything a criminal investigator saw, what he discovered when seeking for the traces of the villains and especially how he discovered them based on their "words", could not have become known to the law workers. A good criminal investigator (I mean the technician and the forensic expert) must know and practise macro photography, micro photography, infrared and ultraviolet photography.

First of all, he must like photography as the poet likes to write; in no way would he ask somebody else to transcribe for him what he thinks is poetry. I know that I will be judged as lacking modesty, but I think that my appraisal was due to the ingenious way in which I have photographically illustrated my research works on site and I have demonstrated the conclusions in the forensic expertises I have done. The forensic photographs, as images of the examined items, must "speak for themselves", the explanations written about them often help. The criminal investigator knows this truth and his photographs prove his good training.

I have seen many works of forensic expertise and illustrations of on-site investigation performed by some of my colleagues and I can say that there were few cases where the photos were unable to say by themselves what they represented.

I must mention that one of my colleagues in forensics has surpassed me in terms of the very good quality of photos. The photographs taken by him, both those on site and those who illustrated the expertise he was asked to collaborate, were true scientific research achievements.

Oftentimes, I remember the cases in which I have been appreciated or just mentioned by various experts in the legal field and not only. I will reproduce one of the situations of this kind. In the years prior to 1999, a fire broke out at a steel factory, namely in the slabbing mill. Then, when the flames and the waves of thick smoke came out of the ingnitron rectifier area, all the officials of that time were watching in amazement the firefighters' activity. Those who had failed to extinguish the fire were getting out from the fire area almost suffocated.

The smoke with a heavy and hot odor had burned their lungs, although they were wearing suits and protection masks. The chief inspector ordered me "to do what I know as a criminal specialist" in investigating this fire. There was no special team appointed to do the on-site research and I had no one to consult or coordinate my activity with. I went down (I was dressed in blue overalls) from the place where we were all looking, on a concrete platform near a railway and I started photographing what I saw. After a few minutes, I was scolded by a man of those who accompanied the officials.

"You, with the camera! Are you not ashamed to take pictures? Who are you?"

I looked at my boss asking him by my glance how to react. He made a short movement of the head, pushing his chin forward as if he were saying, "Do your job and ignore him." I thought it was good to enlighten the one who had questioned me and among the railways I told him in a loud voice who I was and what I was doing. All those on the platform who heard my answer had no reaction. Later, I learned that the man in question was the director of lamination factories.

The fire was extinguished until late at night. In the spotlight, the hall of the ingnitrons looked like a nightmare landscape where an alien cosmic ship had burned. All I did was to photograph as a whole and on parts what was left of the ignitrons, which I compared to some termite mounds, over which chemical smelling pitch had been poured; if you smelled these strongly, they would burn your nostrils and mouth.

After two days, the chief inspector asked me if I made the photos from the slabbing mill. I wanted to show them but he stopped me by telling:

"Go to the scene of the fire where two officers from the capital are waiting for you. They are experts in the matter and you will continue the investigation together.

Only then there was a research team on site where I, the criminal investigator, did not know what to look for; it was the two young engineers whom I found in the basement in the first laminator stand that knew what to do. There was a layer of "cables" coming from the ignitron hall, going to the engines that spun the rollers connected to the incandescent slabs. There, the engineers who were sitting on their bellies like in a trench (on the belly and crawling I reached them, too) showed me a sphere, bigger than a man's head that joined the electrical cables. I realized there was a giant formation of droplets that had occurred among the high power cables. The engineers asked me to photograph it and then to make other frames after they explained to me how the fire had occurred.

"In simple terms for you, as you said you saw tiny pearls, the fires you say the police are investigating, there, the consumption doubles. Do you see those big rolls in front of the stand?"

"They are spinned by two electric engines, these, which are like two four-storey blocks each. They spin those long, thick axes. These engines are powered by the rectified current from the ignitrons in the room you came through. The cables, you saw it, are as thick as your hand. They are aluminum multi-wired with metal, textile and plastic insulation. To reach the engines, they are placed on rackings that are metallic, too. Due to the trepidation, when the 30 ton incandescent slebs went over, the cables rubbed over time, until the insulation was torn and the cables coming together produced a short circuit.

"I imagine that these" short circuited " cables behaved like huge nickel threads."

"It's true! The fire spread over the entire length of the cables burning everything, first of all the plastic insulation."

After I had finished photographing the "cable" layers, the huge droplet effect, the engines, puzzled, I asked the two engineers if such a short circuit could be predicted and prevented.

"It could, if the compulsory checks had been made, but … the production was ongoing and obtaining increased productions of flat laminates made them shorter, so that the resumption of production would be faster.

When I left the flatting mill I saw that the ignitron hall was free, clean with white, freshly painted walls. It had nothing in common with the one in which the fire had taken place. More for me and not for the needs of the investigation I had completed, I photographed the situation at that point. As if understanding my thoughts, the engineers talking to each other were saying: I think they will give up the old solution and will replace the ignitrons. I did not understand anything then and did not ask for clarification.

With the photographs taken, we prepared, according to the forensic rules, sheets that I handed over to the team that investigated the case.

A few months after these events, I was called to the chief inspector's office - where I had a short dialogue:

"Tomassi, I called you to tell me how I can convince someone that in the case of the mill fire it was a technical issued and not a crime!"

"Explain how the short circuit of the cables that feed the engines from the roller track has occurred!" I tried to clarify it.

"No, not like that! I would like to show him the photos you took on site."

"I think I should make another photographic plate."

" I cannot show the photographic plate to the one I want to show my pictures and explanations."

"Who is the one that cannot look at a photo plate and listen to your explanations at the same time? " I asked.

The colonel looked at me in silence and after a while he continued:

"The minister is to come to analyze how it was possible to have a fire broke out burst in the factory. You understand that I have to support my conclusions and be convincing."

I understood and realized that the situation could turn dangerous if the explanations were not convincing.

"I propose, I continued after a while, to exhibit the photos of 1/0.5m in the places where they were taken. You have to give these explanations when it is right where the fire happened. I will make the photos in these sizes, I will frame them and they will be placed where the situation is different now. The walls were painted, everything was cleaned and the ignitrons were installed.

"Well, we will do it! You make some copies of the on site photos. Write explanations for each, too. I'll send someone to take them. Go on!"

The work I did was difficult because I had to zoom the images to the required sizes. The difficulty was that I didn't have trays of 1/1 m. It was difficult, but I made it. I succeeded but my boss back then succeeded, too. I understood it when, although it was a day off, I was called by the officer on duty. When I arrived at the Inspectorate headquarters, the on duty officer informed me that the head of the inspectorate, who was on his way, ordered me to wait for him in the waiting room of his office. I didn't know why I was called; I thought he might order something related to my work, but it wasn't that. When he entered the unit, I saw that he got off his car. He was wearing a long-sleeved white shirt, and tie.

He took his vest from the car, put it on and I saw seeing the signs on his vest I knew he had been promoted. Arriving in the office, he invited me in, where I dared to congratulate him on the promotion. He thanked me and invited me to sit on one of the chairs. Without saying anything, he took out a bottle of whiskey, with two glasses, poured a little from it and offered me one of them, telling me:

"Cheers, Tomassi!"

"Cheers, sir!"

"Your photographs were convincing."

"Thank you!"

"Well, now let's go home."

***

FORENSIC OPINIONS ON THE "EAGLE CASE"

FORENSIC OPINIONS ON THE "EAGLE CASE"

What is shown below represent my opinions about a difficult case of serial killer that has shocked public opinion and not only. I remember, at that time, the fact that the Police Criminal Investigation Institute from all over the country, ordered all the forensic offices in each state, to identify in our records, suspects who could have been the authors of the rapes followed by the death of the victims with the following MO: the author, a man (without description, without ID or identification data) during the night, in dark places, without traffic, on unlit streets and parks, follows (without being seen) women who walk alone through these places; the victims are hit in the head with hard objects, bringing them into a state of unconsciousness; the author has sexual intercourse with the victims in such states, abandoning them in those places.

The order demanded to report the result of the verifications urgently, with reference to the case with the code name "Neptune". We did the checks as asked, without identifying suspects with this operating mode.

If after a short period we would be asked about the result of the ongoing checks, in this case, nobody asked anything. I do not know what the other state forensic offices communicated, but when we asked about the completion of the "Neptune" case we did not receive any answer.

A long silence was kept around this case. I found out, off record I can say, that the solution was due to a group of officers from the Judicial Department and experts from the Criminal Institute, who identified the author together, in the person of a student from the Faculty of Veterinary Medicine in the capital.

From the discussions I had with my superiors in the Criminal Institute, it could be understood that the merit for the author's identification is due to the special quality of the investigation that was carried out on site in the last case.

It was revealed that due to the carefulness and skill of those who carried out the investigation near the victim's body a fragment of rectangular paper was discovered, which was examined under UV rays; it was discovered that the paper was a fragment of a medical prescription: a rectangular stamp was printed on it. The experts established what was the registration number of the doctor who issued the prescription.

This way, the criminal was identified. I was proud of this achievement until I found out, that things were not as I thought. The following was reported on a TV channel:

"The driver of the vehicle who transported the body of the last victim to the Forensic Institute in the capital presented a piece of paper, saying he had raised it from the ground in the place where the victim was found. Because it was wet, he was told to put it on the heater in the room to dry. After it had dried, they noticed it was a fragment of a prescription. This piece of information was transmitted to those of the Criminal Investigation Institute, who later came and took it. ”

This is the truth regarding the "carefulness and skill" of those who did the on site investigation. I was thinking about the multiple investigation cases of crimes committed in a state, when officers came from central offices with "an air of superiority" ordered us and guided us on how to proceed. The vast majority were truly professionals, but unfortunately, there were others who did nothing but take the credit for solving cases.

I do not want to give names, but I was not impressed at all by such specialists as those in the Eagle case. The driver of the Forensic Institute has the credit. I don't know if someone thanked him, but I am doing it now.

The dactyloscopy had special value in this case, which was demonstrated by Francis Galton. The dermatoglyohics is the domain of dactyloscopy that helps to establish the truth, namely that any person has similarities of papillary drawings with the papillary drawings of the parents.

The author of this prestigious achievement was the one who led between the two world wars, the tenprint records of the Capital Police. He is the one who also organized the monoprint record of criminals. Based on it, it was possible to identify with more efficacy the criminals who had left their fingerprint traces on site.

Apart from these scientific concerns, he was a dactyloscopy expert who carried out on-site research in the case of murders with unknown authors committed in the capital.

In his memoirs he recalls the fact that he raised from the site, in the case of two rapes followed by the death of the victims, fingerprint traces of the author who was unknown due to the war conditions of that time.

As a fan of the dactyloscopy, he had kept the traces of those cases in his personal archives. After decades, when he was working within the Forensic Institute in the capital, he would fingerprint the bodies that were brought there for different reasons.

In a certain situation, he was fingerprinting a corpse that had been brought in. It had been found on the railway.

On examining its finger impressions compared to the traces in his personal archives, he found that the person had created the fingerprints raised from the scene in the case of the two rapes, many years before, with unknown authors.

The surprise was huge when the identification data of the corpse were read. He was called R.F. The subsequent investigation established that he was the father of R.I., the murderer who was a student in the Faculty of Veterinary Medicine in the capital.

A criminological truth comes out from these facts. This is the case that can demonstrate Caesare Lombrozo's theory, a man who claimed that criminal children are born from criminal parents.

However, such a conclusion cannot be drawn only from a single case. In order to become a criminal, a man must live in an environment of such type, biological factors having a favorable effect in this respect.

I also say this as R. I., before being executed, shouted that his father was guilty for that. These aspects were not studied from a criminological point of view.

A study on this case could have highlighted the role of genetic inheritance in the genesis of murder.

It could have also highlighted the determining role of the lack of education, of the distortion of sexual instinct which if not monitored and analyzed towards normal behaviors, leads irretrievably to committing highly violent offenses, as the two R. demonstrated – father and son.

***

15
THE
LAST CASE

THE LAST CASE

Forensics is quite a young science. New discoveries in various fields of human knowledge are adapted to fulfilling the purpose of this science: person identification. No other science has such a purpose. This is possible because every object, phenomenon or person may be similar to others, but identical only to themselves. As an element of novelty, I can mention the identification of any person due to the deoxyribonucleic acid, known as DNA.

The method was used for the first time in England, in the 5th decade of the last century, to identify a rapist by examining the semen collected from the victim.

In the practice of modern forensics the way of identifying the objects used in committing crimes, known under the name "interpretation of traces" appeared, but it passed almost unobserved. The interpretation of traces is the subject of a specialized work, creation of my friend, Baldwin.

Through this process, many criminal cases that seemed mysterious and unsolved were elucidated. The paper is the fruit of an experience of more than three decades of forensic expertise in the field of traceology, few people have their say.

The case I describe below is the last of my profession of criminal investigator solved based on the interpretation of the traces. In the summer of 2009, I thought I would retire.

There was a criminal case with unidentified authors, in which an old villager from a village in the north, was found dead on the road that connected two villages.

The investigations carried out left room for interpretations regarding the competence to solve the case. The officers of the judicial service considering the cause of death (cranial bones fracture by a strong blow applied on the forehead with a hard circular object) thought that traffic officers were able to solve the case.

The motivation they used, in addition, was that the body of the deceased had no other traces, and next to it there was a bicycle with deformed wheels.

The officers in the Traffic Department claimed it was a murder because at the place where the body was found there were no traces of tyres, scraps of shards, paint, oil spots as it usually happens on such events.

"Please, Mr. Tomassi, deal with this case."

I replied that I was pleased to do it, and the next day, the teams of the two departments went to the site for an experiment.

I established this experiment after studying the case file. I carefully examined the photos taken at the autopsy, I read the forensic report prepared on this occasion and I found that the only lesion was the circular one on the forehead.

When I arrived at the scene, I saw that the road was on a slope, and the ditches on the two margins were filled with uncut grass. The bicycle had been brought there and put in the position in which it was found on the date the event was announced.

There were many villagers on the arable land on the edges of the road, who, finding out what was going to happen, became very curious.

I realized that it would have been quite difficult to keep everyone away. I preferred to asking them to sit quietly on the edge of the ditch, without staying in our way when carrying out the experiment.

While we were examining the declivity of the road, the way the bicycle wheels looked like (as if there were two big bowls on which a thick tree trunk fell) I heard the cries of a man: stop the horses and come back! What had happened?

A wagon drawn by two horses was coming down from the village. Probably the charioteer did not know what we were doing there. Looking in the direction of the wagon, I saw and heard him pulling the hinges with the "brr, brr" urge, stopped the horses that seemed to be pushed from behind by an unseen force.

At that moment I saw how the drawbar of the wagon rose a lot to the height of the non-commissioned officer who had stopped the wagon.

In that moment I sensed how the "so-called murder" was committed. Interpreting the place and shape where the injury of the deceased was found, I came to the conclusion that the event was actually carried out as follows: during the night, the victim was going up to the village held the bicycle handlebar.

Because it was dark, a wagon similar to the one stopped by the non-commissioned officer, while descending hit him in the forehead with the drawbar of the wagon.

The wagon passed with its rubber wheels over the bike fallen on the asphalt. I thought that probably the one who was driving the wagon involved in the accident left the place sheltered by darkness, continuing its way. Back to the police headquarters in the village, I discussed my hypothesis with the officers of the two departments.

They all agreed that the event occurred as I said. The head of the traffic service then told us that to support of our hypothesis, there is also a piece of information that he had recently got.

"A villager, the owner of a wagon with rubber wheels, would have replaced the drawbar with a new one."

It was natural to go urgently and check the information. It was confirmed that the change took place. I had already clarified who are those competent with solving the case with unknown authors. In a short period of time, the activities of investigation and forensic expertise clarified the veracity of the experiment.

I found out later that the solution given in that case was one of the non-commencement of the criminal prosecution because the deed did not meet the essential features of an offense.

***

9 798224 763030